The Naughtiest Children I Know

Edited by Anne

Illustrate

A Red Fox Book

Published by Random House Children's Books
20 Vauxhall Bridge Road, London SW1V 2SA

A division of The Random House Group Ltd
London Melbourne Sydney Auckland
Johannesburg and agencies throughout the world

1 3 5 7 9 10 8 6 4 2

First published in Great Britain
by Red Fox 2000

Printed and bound by CPI Antony Rowe, Eastbourne

THE RANDOM HOUSE GROUP Limited Reg. No. 954009

www.randomhouse.co.uk

ISBN 0 09 940866 X

This book is for all the children I know
from A to Z
who are good most of the time,
And especially for
AMELIA and EDMUND CHERRY.

And also for that very good grown up
COLIN WEST
who enjoys Cautionary Tales as much as I do.
With love

A. H.

Contents

Contents

Contents

Contents

Contents

Contents

Introduction

The very first Cautionary Tale that I knew was 'The Story of Augustus who would not have any Soup'. I was about 9 and it was in my school poetry anthology, *For Your Delight*. That poem did delight me and didn't alarm me at all. Even though I was a skinny child, unwilling to eat up all the food that the adults insisted was 'good for you' I never believed that Augustus was 'like a little bit of thread' on the fourth day of not eating his soup or that 'on the fifth day he was dead'! Somehow, although many poems about naughty children and their downfalls could be, in real life, very serious, the way they are written gives them a funny slant.

It was much later that I learnt about Heinrich Hoffmann, the German doctor who wrote, in 1845, a whole book of such verses under the title *Struwwelpeter* (in English *Shockheaded Peter*) to amuse his small son, and as a rather joky, sarcastic answer to some earlier, preachy Victorian poems. The Victorians were rather keen on doling out warnings and reminders and strong punishments!

> *Listeners never hear any good of themselves.*
> *Don't lean against the carriage door you'll be thrown out.*
> *There! What did I tell you!*
> *You were told not to go near the fire!*
> *Never put pins in your mouth! Remember what happened to Edith!*

Introduction

Don't touch! Don't look! Don't move!
Do not speak until you are spoken to.
Children should be seen and not heard!
Have you washed your hands, both of them?
Have you a clean pocket handkerchief?
Have you been you know where before you go out?

(I must tell you here that the Red Fox team who worked on this book . . . my editor, Charlie Sheppard, her assistant Ellen Rossiter and Simon Davis in Design . . . never had to be reminded about any of the above; they were all beautifully behaved.)

One poem in *Shockheaded Peter* does seem more scary than the rest: 'The Story of Little Suck-a-Thumb'. Many adults go pale and shaky at mere mention of the title, recalling their first encounter with it in childhood. I've included it, anyway, as I'm sure today's readers are made of sterner stuff.

The poem that actually gave me the idea for this anthology was 'Alice, who had a bad habit of throwing things'. Zöe Barber was only 11 when I chose her poem as winner of a poetry writing competition at Wycombe Abbey School. It made us all laugh and soon had me re-reading such familiar poems as Hilaire Belloc's 'Matilda, who told dreadful lies and was burned to d513465123456798eath . . . ' (not included in this book; in fact you'd be amazed at the number of naughty Matildas in poems – Thomases, Janes and Williams too!) Soon I was searching in libraries and picking other people's brains for ideas, until I discovered some unusual, out of print poems, long-forgotten and ready for a new generation of readers.

And so the collection grew, covering a period of time from 1830 to 2000. Once I'd decided to arrange the poems alphabetically it was plain that they would be unevenly balanced, and I refused to be tied down to the same number of names for each letter. I'm telling you this now so that I don't get complaints about an excess of As, Js and Ms and a scarcity of Zs, Xs and Qs. I expect that you'll notice that some authors appear frequently; having unearthed some neglected poets, hidden away in dusty old books, I wanted to bring them into the light again. You'll see at the back when different writers were writing, and realise how styles and subjects have changed from the 19th to the 21st Century.

On the whole, though, naughtiness goes on in much the same way, and we've all been bad, wild, rude, greedy and disobedient at some time. Instead of telling you stories of some awful things that I did (my grand-daughter asked if I was 'screaming Annie' on page 33!); I'll end with a verse by a Victorian writer, Edward Abbott Parry. He was also a judge so he should know!

> Though children can be rude and wild,
> It's honester to own up,
> I've never known a naughty child
> As naughty as a grown-up.

Anne Harvey, 2000

Extremely Naughty Children

By far
The naughtiest
Children
I know
Are Jasper
Geranium
James
And Jo.

They live
In a house
On the Hill
Of Kidd,
And what
In the world
Do you think
They did?

They asked
Their uncles
And aunts
To tea,
And shouted
In loud
Rude voices:
'We

Are tired
Of scoldings
And sendings
To bed:
Now
The grown-ups
Shall be
Punished instead.'

They said:
'Auntie Em,
You didn't
Say "Thank You"!'
They said:
'Uncle Robert.
We're going
To spank you.'

They pulled
The beard
Of Sir Henry Dorner
And put him
To stand
In disgrace
In the corner.
They scolded
Aunt B.,
They punished
Aunt Jane;
They slapped

Aunt Louisa
Again and again.

They said
'Naughty boy!'
To their
Uncle
Fred
And boxed
His ears
And sent him
To bed.

Do you think
Aunts Em
And Loo
And B.,
And Sir
Henry
Dorner
(K.C.B.),
And the elderly
Uncles
And kind
Aunt Jane
Will go
To tea
With the children
Again? *

* Unlikely, A. H

Elizabeth Godley

Alice
who had a bad habit of throwing things

Alice was a naughty girl,
At her mother she would hurl,
Toys and dishes, glasses too,
Creepy-crawlies from the loo,
Even paper, bits of string,
She would throw most anything.
A letter came addressed to Alice,
From a courtier at the palace.
We need a girl, the letter read,
Pretty, brainy and well-bred,
To be in waiting to the Queen.
Alice, her ambition seen,
Brushed her hair, put on her tights
(The special ones for Friday nights)
And hastened out with quite a fuss,
Missed the train but caught the bus,
All the way to Trafalgar Square,
Because the Queen lives near to there.
As she walked along the Mall,
She met a sentry (very tall).
She said, 'Hello, my name is Alice,
And here's my letter from the palace,
My appointment is right here and now.'
The sentry smiled and gave a bow.

A footman came up, dressed in black,
He said, 'Now madam, round the back,
Tradesman's entrance, in you go,
The job is not yours yet, you know!'
Alice's interview didn't last,
It was all over rather fast.
She sat down quietly for tea,
With plate and napkin on her knee,
But the strain was just too great,
She smashed her cup and broke her plate.
Seeing the best china gone,
Fergie burped and threw a scone,
And soon more plates were in the air
And bread and butter everywhere,
The corgis growled and then joined in,
Charles was bitten on the shin.
The Queen came in and ate a biscuit
Alice felt that she could risk it
And threw a roll shaped like a rose
That hit Prince Philip on the nose.
'That's it!' The Queen was heard to say,
'The Tower for you, and straight away!'
So red-faced Alice in floods of tears
Was put in prison for ten years.

The moral of the tale is this:
At tea with royals – AIM TO MISS!

Zoë Barber

The Story of Augustus
who would not have any Soup

Augustus was a chubby lad;
Fat ruddy cheeks Augustus had:
And everybody saw with joy
The plump and hearty, healthy boy.
He ate and drank as he was told,
And never let his soup get cold.
But one day, one cold winter's day,
He screamed out, 'Take the soup away!
O take the nasty soup away!
I *won't* have any soup to-day.'

Next day, now look, the picture shows
How lank and lean Augustus grows!
Yet, though he feels so weak and ill,
The naughty fellow cries out still,
'Not any soup for me, I say:
O take the nasty soup away!
I *won't* have any soup to-day.'

The third day comes: Oh what a sin!
To make himself so pale and thin.
Yet, when the soup is put on table,
He screams, as loud as he is able,

'Not any soup for me, I say:
O take the nasty soup away!
I WON'T have any soup to-day.'

Look at him, now the fourth day's come!
He scarcely weighs a sugar-plum;
He's like a little bit of thread,
And, on the fifth day, he was — dead!

Heinrich Hoffmann

Quiet Fun

My son Augustus, in the street, one day,
  Was feeling quite exceptionally merry.
A stranger asked him: 'Can you show me, pray,
  The quickest way to Brompton Cemetery?'
'The quickest way? You bet I can!' said Gus,
And pushed the fellow underneath a bus.

Whatever people say about my son,
He does enjoy his little bit of fun.

Harry Graham

Amelia Mixed the Mustard

Amelia mixed the mustard,
  She mixed it good and thick;
She put it in the custard
  And made her Mother sick,
And showing satisfaction
  By many a loud huzza
'Observe,' said she, 'the action
  Of mustard on Mamma.'

A. E. Housman

Arthur

Arthur with a lighted taper
Touched the fire to grandpa's paper.
Grandpa leaped a foot or higher,
Dropped the sheet and shouted, 'Fire!'
Arthur, wrapped in contemplation,
Viewed the scene of conflagration.
'This,' he said, 'confirms my notion –
Heat creates both light and motion.'

Wallace Irwin

Alexander Phillinoy
Who Suffered a Severe Blow

A most revolting little boy
Was Alexander Phillinoy
Who, from his very early years,
(Without tuition, it appears)
Developed with alarming zeal
A habit not at all genteel,
Yet one which I must now disclose:
Young Alexander *picked his nose*,
(The subject is distasteful, yes)
And Alex did it to excess.
At breakfast-time, at lunch, at tea
(*Especially* in company)
Whenever *any*body looked
His thumb and finger would be hooked
Within the left . . . or right . . . hand hole;
And there he'd burrow like a mole.
He didn't care who saw him do it . . .
Picked it, scraped it, never blew it.
His parents did the best they could . . .
They smacked his hands; it did no good.
They told him it was not polite;
It was a truly *awful* sight.
They told him that a handkerchief
Was often used to bring relief
And that this small receptacle
Would help to hide the spectacle

(Which, quite apart from being rude,
Put both his parents off their food).
The more they pleaded and implored
The more young Alexander clawed
And scoured inside the dark abyss
Which was his nasal orifice . . .
And what was more obscene and vile
Was watching Alexander while
He looked at what he'd excavated,
Licked it, liked it, and then ATE it.
At length his father groaned, 'Enough!
Here, Alexander, take some snuff!'
He begged his son on bended knees:
'Inhale it . . . it will make you sneeze.
And here's a handkerchief in case
You feel the urge to wipe your face.'

Young Phillinoy could not resist:
He scooped
a pile
up in his fist
And sniffed the snuff up in a trice
(A hundred grammes to be precise).
He stuffed the lot up all at once
Accompanied by snorts and grunts.

ATCHOO!!
His father cried, 'God Bless!'
And then, 'Oh dear, dear! What a mess!'
ATCHOO!! A-A-T-CHOO!!!' And then 'O Lor!'

For, red and shiny
On the floor
There lay a sight at which they froze:
Alas! 'twas Alexander's nose.
His Dad gasped, 'Holy Moses, son!
You had
two nostrils . . .
now there's one!'
And sure enough, as black as coal,
There was, between his eyes, a hole.

His nose is now not on his face
But in a glass museum case.
It's mounted, with a silver plate
Inscribed: 'Presented to the Tate
By Alexander Phillinoy
Who Used to Use It as a Toy'. . . .
A terrifying sight that's not
By any easily forgot.

Jeremy Nicholas

Adolphus

Adolphus is despicable –
Before the day begins,
To prove that I am kickable,
He kicks me in the shins.

Colin West

Andrew's Bedtime Story

I told him a tale that I adore
Called *Theseus and the Minotaur,*
Of how a prince with a ball of wool
  That his girl friend Ariadne gave him,
Was forced to search for a fiery bull
  Through cave and labyrinth. Keen to save him,
She said, 'Unwind the wool as you go
Through the twisting corridors down below,
And return to me safe – I love you so.'

That was the start of the tale I told,
And Andrew listened, as good as gold.

Next day when he ran home from school,
He found a skein of his mother's wool,
Unwound it, tied it to door and chair,
Along the passage and up the stair,
  Yes, everywhere.
  I opened the door of my room
  To find
Pitschi the cat with his legs entwined,
Jane and Helen flat on the floor,

Great-aunt almost sliced at the knees
(As wire at the grocer's slices cheese),
  All of them trapped.
  The thread I snapped,

With scissors and knife I hacked away
  And set them free.
  But where was A?
There, in a corner lurking, laughing.
  'No more
  Of Ariadne's thread,
My boy,' I cried, 'or we'll all be dead!'
  I stalked away.

But a murderous thread not seen before
Tripped me up, and I cracked my head.

Ian Serraillier

Little Arty

Little Arty at the party
Ate up every single smartie.
After that I saw him take
The hugest slice of chocolate cake.

His glass he filled with something fizzy;
Then keeping Jenny's mother busy,
Asked if he could please take back
That jelly just refused by Jack.

In bed that night his tight pyjamas
Let him know, too much can harm us.
And, after all, when some are needy,
Isn't it dreadful to be greedy?

Jimmy Garthwaite

The Story of Anthony,
The Boy Who Knew Too Much

Anthony, though not unkind,
Had a disbelieving mind.
At a pantomime or play
Anthony would yawn and say,
'Let's go home . . . for I perceive
This is merely make believe.'
When his mother came and read
Story-books to him in bed
Anthony would shake his head:
'Mother, dear, I've had enough
Of this wishy-washy stuff.
If it's all the same to you
Kindly read me something TRUE.'
So his mother, with a sigh,
Meekly laying fiction by,
Read him books about machines,
And scientific magazines.

Christmas time came round once more.
See him sitting on the floor
At a party, after he
Has enjoyed a sumptuous tea.
Solemnly the conjuror stands
Spreading out his empty hands:
Then from nose and ears he hands
Half a dozen billiard-balls,
Shows them with a smile, and then
Makes them disappear again.
Children clap him with a will:
Only Anthony sits still,
Saying loudly, 'I believe
That he's got them up his sleeve.'

The Conjuror, who must have heard
Looked at him, but said no word.

So with all his other tricks:
Flour and butter he would mix
In a bowl, and, 'One . . . two . . . three!'
There the finished cake would be.
Loud applause . . . but Anthony
Merely said, 'Well, I believe
That he had it up his sleeve.'

Coins he'd find in Susan's hair
Which she didn't know were there;
Handkerchiefs of every hue
He would draw from Edward's shoe,

And produce, as pat as pat,
Rabbits from an empty hat.
All the other girls and boys
Laughed and clapped with merry noise:
But Anthony said, 'I believe
He had the whole lot up his sleeve.'

The Conjuror politely smiled
At the infuriating child,
And said, 'Come close, my little man,
And learn my secrets if you can.'
Young Anthony marched up with glee
Remarking, 'Huh! You can't catch *me*!'
'Now,' said the great man, 'one-two-three!'
And Anthony . . . ah, where was he?

His mother wildly glanced around
The boy was nowhere to be found:
But in the Conjuror's top-hat
A third and extra rabbit sat . . .

Children, when you go to parties
Never talk like little smarties:
Even if you *don't* believe,
Keep your knowledge up your sleeve.

Jan Struther

Alonzo
Never-shut-the-door

In vain Alonzo's parents did
All they could think of to remind him,
In vain they punished and they chid –
He never shut a door behind him.

One evening no one was about,
The cook and maids upstairs were stopping,
Father and Mother both were out
And Nurse had gone to do some shopping.

Alonzo coming home that day
With all his thoughts on supper centred,
Left, in his usual careless way,
The street door open when he entered.

The house a passing burglar spied;
His eyes with silent rapture glistened
To see the door set open wide –
And first he stopped outside and listened.

Then stealing in, he smiled to find
Alonzo in a dreadful fluster.
He quickly tied his hands behind
And in his mouth he crammed a duster.

His many-bladed knife he took,
His silver watch ('twas most unpleasant)
A sixpence and a picture book
Just given him — a birthday present.

Then, having other work in view,
The burglar cheerfully departed
And, as good burglars always do,
He shut the door before he started.

In vain did poor Alonzo try
To burst his bonds, which hurt him sadly;
His mouth was full, he could not cry
Or call for help he wanted badly.

In his direction no one passed,
Of duster or of cord to rid him,
Until, returning home at last,
His parents entered and undid him.

Now all is changed, for everywhere
Arriving gently and politely,
Alonzo opens doors with care
And shuts them all behind him, tightly.

W. Trego Webb

Augustus Flatnose

Augustus had a little cot
In which to rest his infant head;
There at some hour, I don't know what,
He every day was put to bed.

Of iron bars the cot was made,
Its sides were very steep and high;
For naughty children aren't afraid
To climb their beds, and often try.

Though nurse had often told him not,
Augustus didn't care a pin.
One day she laid him in his cot,
Pulled up the sheet and tucked him in;

Out walked the nurse and shut the door –
Augustus slyly winked his eye.
'I'll have a climb,' he thought, 'before
That nasty nurse comes back to pry.'

He knew 'twas wrong, but did not stop;
He caught the bars and grasped them well.
With joy he clambered to the top –
Then, tumbling over, down he fell!

He sprawled and screamed upon the mat;
They picked him up, a sight to see,
And found his nose extremely flat –
Much flatter than a nose should be.

Nurse pulled to make its flatness less;
His anxious mother did the same;
His father pulled without success,
And then at last the doctor came.

He pincers to the nose applied,
Which hurt it very much indeed;
Then twisted it from side to side
And in the end it made it bleed.

But something followed worse than that:
For soon the doctor did explain –
'This nose is permanently flat
And NEVER will be round again!'

W. Trego Webb

Screaming Annie

Now listen, children, while I tell
What naughty Annie once befell,
Who always used to cry and rave
So oft as Ma the house would leave.

Quoth, once, Mama: 'Now, Annie, dear,
Be good while I'm away from here.'
But Annie 'gan to storm and flout
And cried: 'I will be taken out!'

Flip, flap, flip, flap . . . what's all this din?
Why, 'tis a stork comes striding in,
A stork with legs both red and thin!
But Annie ceases not to flout,
And 'en begins afresh to shout:
'I will . . . I will be taken out!'

With open beak the solemn stork
Now takes her up as on a fork.
'Flip, flap! nay, never scream and pout,'
Says he: 'you *shall* be taken out!'

Flip, flap, flip flap, away he hies,
Up, up with Annie now he flies;
Within his beak he holds her tight,
Until upon his nest they light.

Instead of cakes, or dainty meat,
She now with storks frog's flesh must eat,
And, willy nilly on the roof
She sadly sits, from all aloof;

For ne'er again might she come down.
And when the summer months had flown,
The stork picked up the child once more,
And through the air his burden bore.

Yes, far away o'er land and sea,
The stork with Annie now doth flee.

Look! high above you see him flying . . .
That comes of naughty children's crying!

Georg Glassbrenner

Untidy Amanda

A naughty child Amanda was;
  She would not comb her hair;
Though it was rough and tangled, too,
  Amanda did not care;
And when Mamma the matted locks
  Would fain have brushed and tied,
Amanda only pushed away
  Her hand, and stamped and cried.

But listen now! It chanced one time
  Mamma had gone away,
Amanda she had left at home
  All by herself that day.
Then someone rattled at the latch;
  Amanda heard him there;
She heard him shutting fast the door
  And creeping up the stair . . .

Someone with scissors in his hand,
  And dreadful gleaming eyes;
'Where is that child who will not comb
  The tangles out?' he cries.
In vain Amanda shrieks and runs,
  He has her by the hair;
Snip-snap! the shining scissors go
  And leave her head quite bare.

Now when Mamma comes home again,
  Ah, what is her surprise
To see Amanda's naked head
  And note her tearful eyes;
And now lest she a cold should catch
  A nightcap she must wear,
And when her locks have grown again
  I'm sure she'll comb her hair.

Kathleen Pyle

Bad Boy Benjamin

Bad Boy Benjamin
Was Very Bad Indeed:
   They told him Tales with Morals that
     He simply wouldn't heed,
       They Spanked him and they Spoke to Him;
       He said He'd Try — and then
         He found a brand new naughtiness —
Bad Boy Ben!

Bad Boy Benjamin,
  Just had to play with Ink,
    He never could remember that
     The Hall was not a Rink,
      He never could remember that
      The Bath was not the Sea,
       And once he broke a PAPERWEIGHT!!!
B—B—B—!

Bad Boy Benjamin,
  He couldn't read or write,
    The goodest thing about him was
     His first-class appetite,
      His only Punctuality was every lunch-time when
      He'd sit him down a Lot Too Soon —
Bad Boy Ben!

Bad Boy Benjamin,
  He mostly Came Down Late,
    He was always Sent Up Early
      As befits a Bad Boy's Fate,
        He wouldn't wait to Answer Back until he'd
                                    counted ten,
        And he wore his pyjams inside-out –
Bad Boy Ben!
HE WORE HIS PYJAMS INSIDE-OUT –
Bad Boy Ben!

Caryl Brahms

Noise

Billy is blowing his trumpet,
Bertie is banging a tin;
Betty is crying for mummy
And Bob has pricked Ben with a pin.
Baby is crying out loudly;
He's out on the lawn in his pram.
I am the only silent one
And I've eaten all of the jam.

James Parker

Bad Belinda

Belinda was a little brat!
The way she teased the dog and cat,
  And even Dickie in his cage,
  Would put you in a perfect rage.
Her mother hoped she'd soon begin
To see her foolishness and sin,
  But every day, as she grew older,
  She grew much naughtier and bolder.

One night she wakened in the dark,
And heard a tiny little bark,
  Then Fido jumped upon the bed,
  And in most solemn tones he said:
'Oh, bad Belinda, bow-wow-wow,
I'll make you feel unhappy now;
  For every day you think it fine
  To whip me till I cry and whine,
And then you do not heed my moans,
But kick me more and steal my bones.'
When Fido stopped, a soft 'mew, mew'
Was heard, and there sat Pussy too.
She said: 'You naughty, naughty child,

Although I've been so meek and mild
When you have pinched and pulled my tail,
And dipped me in the housemaid's pail,
   And wet my coat that's soft as silk,
   And put hot pepper in my milk,
And burnt my whiskers with a match,
To-night, you wretch, I've come to scratch!'

Then in a cold, unpitying way
Her Dickie-bird was heard to say:
   'Chirp, chirp, Belinda, soon you'll squeal
   For all the pains you've made me feel,
I'll peck your snubby little nose,
And all your fingers and your toes.'

Poor, bad Belinda, what a sight
They made of her that fearful night!
   To children it would be a warning
   If they had seen her in the morning.
Her face was pecked with Dickie's beak,
Her arms, her neck, her hands, her cheek
   And even on her head and forehead
   The scratches there were simply horrid!
And oh, I hardly like to tell
How badly Fido bit as well,
   But Fido, Dick, and Puss are pleased,
   For now they're never hurt nor teased.

Isabel M. Carswell

Mischievous Bartholemew

When little boy, Bartholomew
Had reached the happy age of two,
His mother, with a pleasant look,
Gave him a nice new picture book.

Gently at first, the little boy
Turned the leaves with sober joy,
Admired the stork and zebra rare
And softly stroked the llama's hair.

But soon these simple pleasures grew
Insipid to Bartholomew;
And presently, on mischief bent,
He pulled a lead and made a rent.

The rending noise so new and queer
Was very pleasant to his ear;
He ripped the pages through and through:
Thus naughty was Bartholomew.

He docked the tiger of his tail,
Into ten pieces tore the whale,
Slit the long neck of the giraffe
And split the crocodile in half.

B

Ah, sad it was to see the book
His mother gave, with pleasant look!
His nurse grieved and his mother too –
'I'm sleepy,' said Bartholomew.

Soon in his little room undressed
And put to bed, he could not rest.
In dreams he saw beside his bed
A grim procession – full of dread.

First marched a tail-less tiger, then
A whale arranged in pieces ten;
Next a giraffe, all headless, passed
And two half crocodiles at last.

This dreadful dream the whole night through
Affrighted poor Bartholomew,
All night the beasts with ghostly tread
Stalked up and down beside his bed.

Since then, an altered boy, he tore
His pretty picture books no more;
His nurse is pleased and mother too,
So careful is Bartholomew.

W. Trego Webb

Ill-timed Levity

I scarce can speak, Bartholomew,
I am so much displeased with you
   For all that has ocurr'd:
Aunt Porter, who had come to stay
Has in her chariot roll'd away
   Without a parting word.

Last Night, when all were sent to Dine,
You took a Fish-hook, and some Twine
   And, leaning o'er the stair,
When Honoured Guests went by Below
Let slyly down the Hook, and so
   Secured it in her Hair.

Alas! Aunt Porter, long denied
That crown which is a woman's Pride,
   And thinking, sure, no ill,
At table duly took her seat
With seasoned Majesty replete
   And amiable Good-will.

At last she rais'd her hand appalled
And sudden found that she was Bald,
   And for her speech did strive;
The scene I cannot now pursue,
It has been given to very Few
   Such Moments to survive.

Ah me! You can understand
What pow'r may lie in childish Hand
    E'en at such tender Age.
Our Relative in high Disgust
Will make Resentment, deep and just,
    Our only Heritage.

Violet Jacob

Clumsy Clarissa

Clarissa did the washing up:
She smashed a plate and chipped a cup,
And dropped a glass and cracked a mug,
Then pulled the handle off a jug.
She couldn't do much worse, you'd think,
But then she went and broke the sink.

Colin West

Celia

Celia always took her time
Over what she had to do.
She'd take at least six minutes
Just to fasten up one shoe.

To find her coat would be a task
Of many minutes more.
It could be half an hour
Before Celia reached the door.

'Please hurry' and 'Don't dawdle'
Meant nothing to that child.
Celia always managed
To drive her parents wild.

Fay Maschler

The Story of Cheeky Charles

Now Charles had been brought up with care
At Number 12 Begonia Square
And taught while still extremely young
Not to misuse the English tongue.
No words unfit for him to hear
Had ever reached his sheltered ear . . .
For instance, such disgusting slang
As 'Gosh' and 'Golly', 'Blow' and 'Hang'.
Imagine, therefore, what a pang
His learned father felt one day
When Charles distinctly said, 'Okay.'

'Charles!' cried his father in amaze,
'Where did you learn that vulgar phrase?
Refrain from using it, I pray.'
And meekly Charles replied, 'Okay!'

The horrid habit grew and grew:
It seemed the only word he knew.
Whatever he was asked to do
To eat or drink, to work or play . . .
All Charles could answer was, 'Okay.'

At last his father took him to
That interesting place, the Zoo,
And most politely asked to see
The Head Curator, Mr B.

'I wish,' he said, in accents pleasant,
'To make the Zoo a little present.
Your parrot-house, as I have heard,
Has ample room for one more bird.
Then take, I beg, this creature here,
Whose squawking grates upon my ear.'

'Delighted!' Mr B replied.
'One of our birds has lately died.
I'll just take down his name and age . . .
Keeper! Conduct him to his cage.'

So now, whene'er the weather's fine,
His brothers, Claude and Constantine,
Are brought on Sundays, after Church,
To look at Charles upon his perch.
'Observe, before it is too late,
Your disobedient brother's fate,
And see how vulgar catchwords can
Transform a little gentleman.'
'Yes, yes, Papa,' the boys reply,
While wicked Charles pretends to cry.
But after they have gone away
He cocks his head and screams, 'Okay!'

Jan Struther

Christopher Cash

Now here is the story of Christopher Cash,
    The boy who delighted to break and to smash,
Who spoilt all his own and his playfellows' toys,
Smash! . . . Crash! . . . 'It's Christopher Cash!'
    Exclaim all the girls and the boys.

Sister May with her dolly was playing one day,
When Christopher craftily snatched it away.
    Great holes in her sash he proceeded to slash,
And in spite of the pleadings of poor little May,
    Dolly's head on the fender continued to bash.

The inkpots at school on the floor he would dash,
And exclaiming 'I hate all this stupid old trash!'
    His lesson-books flung far and wide with his might,
'Come, Christopher Cash, I must give you the lash!'
    His Schoolmaster cried, and it served him quite right!

He was walking one day on the cliff by the sea,
    When his mother called out to him, 'Do not be rash!
Don't go near the edge!' – but no notice took he,
    So into the water he fell with a splash,
    A sharp-pointed rock in his head made a gash,
And that was the finish of Christopher Cash!

Katherine E. Sherriff

Cynthia Simpson
Who Stuck it Out to the Bitter End

A habit that is commonplace is
Pulling lots of silly faces.
Cynthia Simpson found that she
Could do this most amusingly.
For once, when she was very young
She found, by sticking out her tongue,
It did not only look quite rude, it
Was so long that it extruded
Right up to her nose's tip
(So handy, when it chanced to drip)
And down to just below her chin.
She hardly ever kept it in
But stuck it out at everyone ...
Her school friends thought it *heaps* of fun.
She'd screw her face up, go cross-eyed
And wag her tongue from side to side,
Then hunch her back, and strike a pose,
Blow out her cheeks and lick her nose,
Or wave her hands and squint and leer
And make her eyeballs disappear –
A kind of facial acrobat.
Her Dad said 'It will stick like that.
You mark my words.' 'Oh phooey, Dad,'
Said Cynthia. But, next day, it had.

If only she had said 'Okay'
She wouldn't have a lisp today.

She findth it hard to thay her name.
Her tongue thtickth out. Ith thuch a shame.
She altho hath to wear a bwathe
To keep pwotwuding teeth in plathe,
And whatth an even gweater pity . . .
Thynthia thtarted out quite pwetty.

Jeremy Nicholas

My Sister Clarissa

My sister Clarissa spits twice if I kiss her
and once if I hold her hand.
I reprimand her – my name's Alexander –
for spitting I simply can't stand.

'Clarissa, Clarissa, my sister, is this a
really nice habit to practise?'
But she always replies with innocent eyes
rather softly, 'Dear Brother, the fact is

'I think I'm an ape with a very small grape
crushed to juice in my mastodon lips.
Since I am not a prude, though I hate being rude,
I am simply ejecting the pips.'

George Barker

The Story of Little Suck-a-Thumb

One day Mamma said, 'Conrad dear,
I must go out and leave you here.
But mind now, Conrad, what I say,
Don't suck your thumb while I'm away.
The great tall tailor always comes
To little boys who suck their thumbs;
And ere they dream what he's about,
He takes his great sharp scissors out,
And cuts their thumbs clean off – and then,
You know, they never grow again.'

Mamma had scarcely turned her back,
The thumb was in, Alack! Alack!

The door flew open, in he ran,
The great, long, red-legged scissor-man.
Oh! children, see! The tailor's come
And caught out little Suck-a-Thumb.
Snip! Snap! Snip! the scissors go;
And Conrad cries out, 'Oh! Oh! Oh!'
Snip! Snap! Snip! They go so fast,
That both his thumbs are off at last.

Mamma comes home: there Conrad stands,
And looks quite sad, and shows his hands;
'Ah!' said Mamma, 'I knew he'd come
To naughty little Suck-a-Thumb.'

Heinrich Hoffmann

Charley, The Story-Teller

Charles was a very wayward youth,
Who to his parents ne'er spoke truth.
It matters not, thought he, forsooth,
When no-one knows; if I tell lies
They are not written in my eyes!

His mother once some questions asked,
And artful Charles his cunning tasked,
When loud the parrot chuckling cried:
'You little rogue! may woe betide!
    For Charley, you've been fibbing!'

Then from the corner comes the cat,
And gives Mama a gentle pat:
She purrs aloud: 'Mew, mew, mew, mew . . .
    For Charley has been fibbing!'

Down stairs now frightened Charley steals,
As tho' ten cats were at his heels;
When by his coat Tray seizes him,
And cries: 'Bow, wow' in accents grim,
    'Fie, Charley, you've been fibbing!'

Now both with shame and anger red,
That e'en the cock and hen upbraid,
He seeks the garden's safe retreat;
But twitt'ring birds there cry: 'Tweet, twee
    'Fie, Charley, you've been fibbing!'

D

He runs at last from out the town,
And in a village sits him down;
But even there a fly soon comes,
Who buzzes round his nose and hums:
  'Fie, Charley, you've been fibbing!'

He now the blessed world runs round,
But rest for him was nowhere found;
Go where he would his ears still greet:
'Mew, mew . . . bow, wow . . . buzz, buzz . . . tweet, tweet!
  Fie, Charley, you've been fibbing!'

Georg Glassbrenner

Deborah Delora

Deborah Delora, she liked a bit of fun –
She went to the baker's and bought a penny bun;
Dipped the bun in treacle and threw it at her teacher –
Deborah Delora! What a wicked creature!

Anon

Dave Dirt Came to Dinner

Dave Dirt came to dinner
   And he stuck his chewing gum
Underneath the table
   And it didn't please my Mum

And it didn't please my Granny
   Who was quite a sight to see
When she got up from the table
   With the gum stuck to her knee

Where she put her cup and saucer
   When she sat and drank her tea
And the saucer and the chewing gum
   Got stuck as stuck can be

And she staggered round the kitchen
   With a saucer on her skirt –
No, it didn't please my Granny
   But it
        PLEASED
          DAVE
            DIRT.

Kit Wright

D

Naughty Dan, the Deceitful Boy

Dan was a bold and wayward youth
Who never stood about the truth,
But when he'd broke a glass or cup,
Quick to his Pa would bustle up,
Say 'twas his sister's fault alone,
And vow that he no harm had done.
Then if Papa his sister struck,
He thought himself in high good luck,
And when he saw her cry and grieve,
He stood by, laughing in his sleeve.

His mother once some apples missed,
When in bounced Dan, and must insist
His sister had the pantry sacked,
For he had caught her in the act!
But lo! his pocket had a hole,
From out of which three apples stole,
And as upon the floor they dropped,
E'en Daniel's tongue for shame was stopped.
So ever after this occurred,
No one believed him on his word.

Dan dared not pilfer now at home,
But oft through orchards would he roam.
One night, on climbing up a tree,
A branch gave way...plump! down fell he!
And caught his foot within a trap!
Loud bawled for help the luckless chap,
But no-one stirred ... the neighbours said:
"'Tis only Dan ... let's keep in bed.'
Thus on himself the tables turned,
A useful lesson Daniel learned.

Julius Baehr

The Story of Disobedient David

Young David was forbidden quite
To play with the electric light,
But when he asked the reason why,
He got this very strange reply:
'Two hundred volts,' his father said,
'Are quite enough to kill you dead.'

'But what *are* volts?' the boy enquired.
'Don't worry, child! Your father's tired.'

Now David, who was rash and bold
And seldom did what he was told,

D

At once determined to find out
What all this fuss could be about.

His pocket-knife he quickly drew
And cut the electric wire in two.

Imprudent boy! A monstrous spark
Flew out at him — then all was dark.
Poor David shrieked in wild alarm,
For through his hand and up his arm
Two hundred raging demons leapt,
And pinched and pricked him till he wept.
Blindly he stumbled from the room:
He could not dodge this dreadful doom.

All over him the demons clung
And mercilessly stabbed and stung;
With horrid glee and fiendish grins
They plied their little red–hot pins.

They drove him, howling, down the stairs
And out into the streets and squares,
And people wondered, as he passed,
How any boy could run so fast.

His parents searched for him in vain:
David was never seen again.
So now they sit (unhappy sight!)
And mourn their loss — by candle-light.

Jan Struther

Dirty Dick

A sadder fate than that of Dick
'Twould puzzle you to find:
He said that water made him sick,
And dirt he didn't mind.

He never washed his hands or face,
Nor had a bath like you;
But dirty went about the place,
And gloried in it too!

At last his parents found one night
(It made them very sad),
In him, with all his dirt, they quite
A kitchen-garden had.

Potatoes from his fingers sprout,
And green stuff from his toes;
And water-cress all round about
His neck and shoulders grows!

Clifton Bingham

D

Porridge

Dorothea, Dolly, Dot,
wouldn't eat her porridge hot.
Left it sitting on the table,
said,
'I'll eat it when I'm able.'

'Eat it now,'
her mother said.
'Or you'll go straight back to bed.'

'NO,'
said one.
'YES,'
Said the other.
'Dorothea I'm your mother
simply do as you are told.'
'No,' said
Dolly Dot.
'It's cold.'

Peggy Dunstan

Envious Eliza

Eliza was an envious Miss,
Who always wanted that or this.

Though she had dollies three or four,
She envied every girl with more.

She sighed for this, she pined for that,
Her cousin's frock, her sister's hat;

No matter what the thing might be,
'I wish I could have that!' said she.

One day when her mother told
Her little sister had a cold,

Cried she, 'Why haven't I one too?'
Which was a silly thing to do.

Eliza caught a cold next day,
In bed a week she had to stay.

Beware of being envious,
Or you, like her, may suffer thus!

Clifton Bingham

Ermyntrude

A little girl called Ermyntrude
Was often curiously rude –
Came down to breakfast in the nude.
Her sister said (though not a prude):
'It seems to me extremely crude
To see your tummy over food:
Your conduct borders on the lewd.
Also, you nastily exude
Cornflakes and milk as though you'd spewed' –
Her lips were open when she chewed,
And read a comic-book called *Dude*.
She was a sight not to be viewed
Without profound disquietude.
Though what could come but such a mood
From anyone named Ermyntrude?

Roy Fuller

Haircutting

The hairdresser came to cut Emily's hair,
Who sat very still all the time in the chair
You see she knows better than stir!
Whilst silly Eliza her night-cap must wear
For finding the scissors she cut her own hair.
So we won't show a picture of her.

Elizabeth Turner

Fidgety Frank

Frank never, never would keep still,
His fidgets made his mother ill.

'Oh, do leave off!' the folks would say,
Or you will fidget right away!'

He wore out holes in all his boots,
And in the knees of all his suits;

With fidgeting he grew so thin,
He soon looked only bone and skin.

At bed-time when he had his bath,
He was no bigger than a lath;

He fidgeted in bed at night,
Until he looked a shadow quite.

Thus bit by bit, from day to day,
He fidgeted himself away;
And now he's got so tiny small,
There's nothing left of him at all!

Clifton Bingham

Felicia Ropps

Funny, how Felicia Ropps
Always handles things in shops!
Always pinching, always poking,
Always feeling, always stroking
Things she has no right to touch!
Goops like that annoy me much!

Gelett Burgess

Fred

Fred borrowed Father's tools one day.
Yes, Father said he could.
He used them in the garden
To build a den of wood.
He promised to be careful,
And put them back again,
But Fred is so forgetful,
He left them in the rain.

Now Father's very angry.
The hammer can't be found,
The screwdriver is missing,
The nails lie on the ground.
The saw is bent and rusty,
It just won't cut a thing.
'Next time,' says Frederick's father,
'You'll fix your den with string.'

Alison Winn

Godfrey Gordon Gustavus Gore

Godfrey Gordon Gustavus Gore –
No doubt you have heard the name before –
Was a boy who never would shut a door!

The wind might whistle, the wind might roar,
And teeth be aching and throats be sore,
But still he never would shut the door.

His father would beg, his mother implore,
'Godfrey Gordon Gustavus Gore,
We really *do* wish you would shut the door!'

Their hands they wrung, their hair they tore;
But Godfrey Gordon Gustavus Gore
Was deaf as the buoy out at the Nore.

When he walked forth the folks would roar,
'Godfrey Gordon Gustavus Gore,
Why don't you think to shut the door?'

They rigged out a Shutter with sail and oar,
And threatened to pack off Gustavus Gore
On a voyage of penance to Singapore.

But he begged for mercy, and said, 'No more!
Pray do not send me to Singapore
On a Shutter, and then I will shut the door!'

'You will?' said his parents; 'then keep on shore!
But mind you do! For the plague is sore
Of a fellow that never will shut the door,
Godfrey Gordon Gustavus Gore!'

William Brighty Rands

Griselda

Griselda is greedy, I'm sorry to say.
She isn't contented with four meals a day,
Like breakfast and dinner and supper and tea
(I've had to put tea after supper – you see
     Why don't you?)
Griselda is greedy as greedy can be.

She snoops about the larder
For sundry small supplies,
She breaks the little crusty bits
Off rims of apple pies,
She pokes the roast potato dish
When Sunday dinner's done,
And if there are two left in it
Griselda snitches one;
Cold chicken and cold cauliflower
She pulls in little chunks –
And when Cook calls:
  'What are you doing there?'
    Griselda bunks.

Griselda is greedy. Well, that's how she feels,
She simply can't help eating in-between meals,
And always forgets what it's leading to, though
The Doctor has frequently told her; 'You know
    Why, *don't* you?'
When the stomach-ache starts and Griselda says:
  'Oh.'

  She slips down to the dining-room
  When everyone's in bed,
  For cheese-rind on the supper-tray,
  And buttered crusts of bread,
  A biscuit from the biscuit-box,
  Lump sugar from the bowl,
  A gherkin from the pickle-jar,
  Are all Griselda's toll;
  She tastes the salted almonds,
  And she tries the candied fruits –
And when Dad shouts:
  'Who *is* it down below?'
    Griselda scoots.

Griselda is greedy. Her relatives scold,
And tell her how sorry she'll be when she's old,
She will lose her complexion, she's sure to grow fat,
She will spoil her inside – does she know what she's at?
    (Why *do* they?)
Some people *are* greedy. Leave it at that.

Eleanor Farjeon

Word of Honour

No power of language can express
The irritation and distress
   It used to be to Mrs Trales
   To see her children bite their nails.

In vain she tied their hands in bags;
They chewed the corners into rags.
   Even bitter aloes proved a waste
   The children grew to like the taste.

So for a week with constant smacks
She bound their hands behind their backs;
   Then said, 'Now promise, George and Jane,
   Never to bite your nails again!'

And when the promise had been wrung
From sobbing throat and stammering tongue,
   She added, with a threatening brow,
   'Mind! You're upon your honour now!'

The votive pair, their spirits bowed,
With sullen looks the claim allowed;
   And 'bound in honour' forth they went
   To try a fresh experiment.

Time passed: till Mrs Trales one day
Remarked in quite a casual way –
   Threading her needle in between –
   'Come, show me if your hands are clean!'

With conscious looks the guilty pair
Adjusted flattened palms in air:
   But she, not meaning to be lax,
   Observed, 'Now let me see the backs!'

Which being shown, there plain to see
Were nails as short as short can be!
   'What?' cried Mamma, her anger stirred,
   'Is this the way you keep your word?'

Then, nerved to desperation, Jane
Cried, 'Wait, Mamma, and I'll explain:
   For bad at first though things appear,
   Indeed it is not as you fear!

'Though at first glance our nails may strike
Your eye as shorter than you'd like,
   Yet, dear Mamma, pray bear in mind
   For weeks they have been much behind!

'And often, when the wish occurred
To bite them, we recalled our word,
   And never, never would we break
   The promise we were forced to make!

'So, now, whenever George or I
Starve for a taste of finger-pie,
   Then turn and turn about we dine –
   First I bite his and he bites mine.'

What happened next you may surmise,
While in between came anguished cries –
'You never did put me or Brother
On honour not to bite each other!'

Laurence Housman

Inconsiderate Hannah

Naughty little Hannah said
   She could make her Grandma whistle,
So, that night, inside her bed,
   Placed some nettles and a thistle.

Though dear Grandma quite infirm is,
   Heartless Hannah watched her settle,
With her poor old epidermis
   Resting up against a nettle.

Suddenly she reached the thistle!
My! you should have heard her whistle.

   ★   ★   ★   ★   ★   ★

A successful plan was Hannah's,
But I cannot praise her manners.

Harry Graham

The Busy Child

Hannah, a busy meddling thing,
Would peep in every place;
A habit which must always bring
Young folks into disgrace.

One day, her mother put a jar
Upon a cupboard shelf;
Sly Hannah viewed it from afar,
And said within herself,

'What can mama have placed so high?
It must be something nice,
And, if I thought she was not nigh,
Would see it in a trice.'

Quick on the table then she skipped,
When feeling some alarm,
She sudden turned, her left foot slipped,
She fell – and broke her arm.

Mary Belson

Kind Aunt Mary

(Papa speaks.)

'Horace, with Shame I have to Speak:
The Cricket Match we had Last Week
Has Prov'd a Source of so much Pain
I shall not Let you Play Again.

'I Marked you, Horace, make your Runs,
The Fleetest Footed of my Sons,
With Benjamin in Trousers Yellow
(A very Manly Little Fellow).

'I saw you Strike the Ball on high,
A Catch that Hover'd in the Sky,
I heard the Universal Shout
And Cheering that Proclaim'd you Out.

'Your Eye sent forth a Furious Glare,
You Hurl'd your Bat into the Air,
And the Spectators and their Wives
With One Accord ran for their Lives.

'You Gnashed your Teeth, you Tore your Braces
And Flung them Right in People's Faces;
Even the Collar of your Shirt
You Rent and Trampled in the Dirt!

'Now Kind Aunt Mary Watch'd the Play
Upon that Most Unlucky Day,
But Kind Aunt Mary's Boots were Tight
And so she could not Join the Flight.

'Alas! the Bat like Lightning Sped,
And Fell like Thunder on her head;
I Thought my Very Heart had Stopp'd
To see how Kind Aunt Mary Dropp'd.

'They Bore her Home upon a Stretcher
(Two of the Gardeners Came to Fetch her),
And I Myself, who Walk'd Beside,
To Both her Nostrils Salts Applied.

'We Bath'd her Brows with Rum and Brandy
And ev'ry Spirit that Was Handy,
Pail After Pail on her I Threw
Of Water Cold, to Bring her To.

'Then Kind Aunt Mary Chok'd and Stirr'd;
And seemed to Struggle for a Word;
When Sev'ral Other Pails I'd Flung,
Then Kind Aunt Mary Found her Tongue.

'She Clench'd her Fists, her Eyes Grew Round,
She said, "I have been Nearly Drown'd."
I Whisper'd, "Pray be Calm and Steady,"
And Got another Pailfull Ready.

'Between her Gasps she Shouted, "Cease!
Or I will Send for the Police!"
(I really Can't Repeat the Rest.)
I said, "I Did it For the Best."

'Then Kind Aunt Mary Rose and said,
"Your Son has Tried to Break my Head
And you have Drench'd me to the Bone,
So Your Acquaintance I Disown.

' "For he is Young and may be Taught,
But you're More Senseless than I thought;
And when Your Doings I Compare,
I think you are the Worst. Beware!"

'Horace, your Deed I do Deplore
For she will Smile on us No More;
Even my Conduct, Just and Wise,
Seems Wrong in Kind Aunt Mary's Eyes.

'Boy, Curb your Wrath – Reflect with Shame
How I have had to Bear the Blame;
Preserve, my Son, through Storm and Shine,
Demeanour Mild and Calm, like Mine.'

Violet Jacob

The Education of Grandpa

Grandpa, in a nursemaid's role
Took small Henry for a stroll.
Henry, when the time was pat,
Poked a stick through Grandpa's hat.
Grandpa, at his childish joke,
Rather petulantly spoke.
'This,' said Henry with contrition,
'Sweetens Grandpa's disposition.'

Henry stretched a wire slack
Right across his Grandpa's track,
Calling sweetly, 'Grandpa dear,
I've a great surprise ... Come here!'
Grandpa, willing to admire,
Came and tripped across the wire,
Henry cried: 'This visitation
Trains your powers of observation.'

Henry, with a care discreet,
Placed a tack upon a seat.
Grandpa, with rheumatic joint,
Sat himself upon the point.
Joyful light filled Henry's eye
When his grandsire leaped on high
'This will teach you readiness ...
Quick response in times of stress!'

Ere this quiet stroll was done
Henry tried another one . . .
Hit his grandpa with a can,
Whereupon that gentleman,
Every aged nerve a-tingle,
Walloped Henry with a shingle.
'Joy!' said Henry 'twixt his cries,
'This gives Grandpa exercise!'

When the skies were all a-gloam
Greybeard man and child strolled home.
Grandpa's limbs were somewhat battered
And his modest clothes were tattered,
And he leaned upon his cane,
Like a being wracked with pain,
But the grandchild's tone was gay,
'Grandpa's learnt a lot to-day!'

Wallace Irwin

Humphrey Hughes of Highbury

Young Humphrey Hughes of Highbury
Goes to his local library;
They stamp his books, he softly speaks,
'I'll bring them back within three weeks.'
He always looks so meek and mild
That grown-ups think, 'There goes a child
Who'll grow into a charming youth.'
But little do they know the truth.

For when he's home, young Humphrey Hughes
Forgets to ever wipe his shoes,
And at his mother merely sneers
As to his room he disappears.
When there his library books he takes,
His body with excitement shakes,
For Humphrey so enjoys himself
When placing books upon his shelf.

But there upon his shelf they stay,
Untouched, unread, until the day
He takes one down and with a grin
Looks at the date that's stamped within.

With laughter he begins to shriek,
For all his books were due last week.
He then decides the thing to do
Is wait another week or two.

So time goes by until, at last,
When six or seven weeks have passed,
There comes the knock upon the door
That Humphrey has been waiting for.
His mother gets a nasty shock
When answering the caller's knock,
For there she finds two boys in blue –
In search of books long overdue.

But, pleading absentmindedness,
Young Hughes could simply not care less
And so, with some reluctancy,
The constables accept his plea.
They take the long-lost books away,
But warn he'll have a fine to pay,
Yet Humphrey merely looks benign,
For Mummy always pays the fine!

Colin West

Henry King
who chewed bits of string, and was
early cut off in dreadful agonies

The Chief Defect of Henry King
Was chewing little bits of string.
At last he swallowed some which tied
Itself in ugly Knots inside.
Physicians of the Utmost Fame
Were called at once; but when they came
They answered, as they took their fees,
'There is no Cure for this Disease.
Henry will very soon be dead.'
His Parents stood about his Bed
Lamenting his Untimely Death,
When Henry, with Latest Breath,
Cried: 'Oh, my friends, be warned by me,
That Breakfast, Dinner, Lunch, and Tea
Are all the Human Frame requires . . .
With that, the Wretched Child expires.

Hilaire Belloc

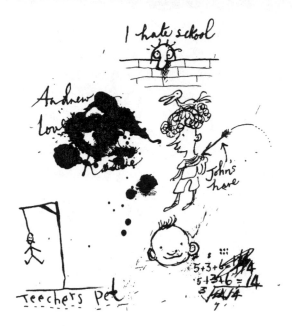

Isaac Beattie

This is the tale of Isaac Beattie
Who covered walls with rude graffiti;
Not only walls, but fences, doors,
Windows, paths and gates and floors.
He never worked when it was light-time
But carried out his 'art' at night-time.
Paint spray beneath his coat, he crept
While unsuspecting victims slept
He dearly loved a white front door
On which to spray red paint like gore.
A postman cried: 'I had to run!
I thought a murder had been done!'

Walls, craftsman made, so old and fine
He targeted: 'Those bricks are mine!'
Many home owners were quite scandalised
To see their property so vandalised.
The neighbourhood went quite ballistic;
Isaac was not at all artistic.
He fooled the Police and Neighbourhood watch,
Each plan to catch him out he'd scotch.
Buses and trains were purest joy
For garish splattering by this boy.
Shop windows, too, he loved to spray,
Completely masking the display.
In fact all places that were 'No Go'
Were blemished by his fiendish LOGO.

One dark night Isaac caused sensation
Down at the local Railway station;
He climbed some railings where a sign
Said; DANGER! DO NOT CROSS THIS LINE!
Too late! With spray can at the ready,
He wobbled, slipped, fell, far from steady,
The spray exploded in his face
Which twisted in a foul grimace.
Paint filled his eyes, leaked down his coat,
Gurgled in ears and nose and throat.
Thus was the end of Isaac Beattie,
A victim of his own graffiti.

Anne Harvey

Lost

Isabella lost things every day,
In school, at home, both outside and inside;
Her teachers all despaired of her . . . in vain!
'One day you'll lose your head!' her mother cried.

On Monday she screamed out: 'I've lost a sock,
And I can't go to school just wearing one.'
Her mother searched and searched, but couldn't find it
So sent her off to school just wearing none.

On Tuesday she yelled: 'Help! I've lost my project!
It's gone . . . the one on Florence Nightingale!
I'll get kept in . . . I've lost my homework too!
Science and maths!' her mother heard her wail.

'And someone's got my lunch-box and my glasses,'
She moaned on Wednesday; 'I can hardly see!
I hope you'll be in after school today,
Or else I can't get in . . . I've lost my key!'

Thursday was a bad day . . . no P. E. Kit,
No trainers in the mess under her bed,
No watch to tell the time, no comb or hairbrush,
Her mother said again, 'You'll lose your head!'

On Friday Isabella's mother heard
Her daughter scream: 'It's lost! And no-one cares!'
And looking up from toast and coffee saw
A headless child come walking down the stairs.

Anne Harvey

Ivor Brown
Who placed too much Reliance on Mechanical Aids,
And was put into an institution.

IVOR BROWN, when a tiny Boy,
Was given an exciting Toy
By his oh! too indulgent Pater –
It was a Pocket Calculator.
The Lad took up the Gift with Glee,
And soon attained Proficiency
In working out what 87
Minus 3 and Plus 11,
Multiplied by 63,
Plus 12% of 8 would be
If it were divided by
Half of the Square Root of π
(And other problems of that Kind,
Which so amuse the Infant Mind).
And, when he'd got the Answer, 'Crumbs!'
He'd cry, 'Oh aren't I Good at Sums!'

He was – and yet it must be said –
He couldn't do them in his Head.
And when at school his teachers tried
To show the Method, IVOR sighed

And sniffed and coughed and scratched his hair
And yawned and SIMPLY DIDN'T CARE!

It happened, though, a Ghastly Fate
Was stalking the Young Reprobate.
He went to spend his Christmas Loot
(A Five-pound Note from Auntie Toot)
In a Large Department Store,
Picked up one Toy and wanted more,
So on his Calculator pored,
To see how much he could Afford.
He added up what he must Pay
And checked the Visual Display,
Which showed – to the delight of IVOR –
That he'd spent Nowhere Near a Fiver.
He took more Toys and more and more,
As if he'd got all he could hold,
He went to the Check-Out and, as Bold
As Brass, he offered up his Fiver
To pay for All – Oh! Wretched IVOR!
He'd chosen to go into Town
The Day his Batteries ran down!

He might have Got Away With It,
If he had not been such a Nit.
The Check-Out Girl asked for more Money.
IVOR said, 'Now don't be funny.

Look – I've given you Five Nicker,
Give me my Change! Come on, Girl, quicker!'
The Girl refused, so IVOR swore,
Picked up his Toys, and left the Store.

The Magistrate, with Eye Severe,
Probationed him for Half a Year,
But Ivor went from Bad to Worse –
Stole his Probation Lady's Purse!
For which Society's Retribution
Put him in an Institution.
And there Poor IVOR, Sad to Say,
Remains until this very Day.

MORAL:
No Machine (of any Sort)
Will ever take the Place of Thought,
And Man – let it be widely known! –
Can't live by Microchip alone.

Simon Brett

The Dreadful Story of Janet

Janet, when she went out shopping,
Had a tiresome trick of stopping
Every yard to point and say,
'Mother, buy me that, I pray!'
First a coat of squirrel's fur . . .
That, she thought, would just fit *her*;
Then, a gown of velvet blue . . .
That would suit her nicely, too;
And this fashionable hat . . .
'Please, Mamma, I *must* have *that*!'

'Tut, my child!' her mother chid.
'Come along as you are bid.
Children nowadays . . . it's funny . . .
Seem to think one's made of money.'
Janet tossed her head and pouted
When her wishes thus were flouted,
And to give Mamma a fright
(Serve the silly creature right!)
Into Horridge's she slipped
While her mother outward tripped.

No one stops her. Up she goes
Till she comes to Children's Clothes;
Sees a cupboard, creeps inside . . .
Just the very place to hide!
Soon Mamma will come and get her,
Hug and kiss and pat and pet her,

And in future dress her better:
(So at least she fondly thinks,
This designing little minx!)

Oh, how slow the hours crawl, . . .
Scarcely seem to move at all.
First she nodded, then she dozed:
When she woke the shop was closed.
Janet . . . a courageous child . . .
Nothing daunted, simply smiled,
Doffed her clothes, and then got dressed
In all the things she liked the best.
There she strutted, bold as brass,
Smirking in the looking-glass,
Till a voice addressed her thus: . . .
'Now, of course, you're one of us.'

Janet, turning in a fright,
Saw a most unnerving sight . . .
Half a dozen waxen brats,
Dressed in costly coats and hats,
Facing her with glassy stare,
Painted cheeks and flaxen hair.
'How d'you do? I'm Simpering Sue.
These ones here are Preening Prue,
Dandy Dick and Mincing Molly,
Namby Nick and Prinking Polly.
Now with us you're bound to stay,
Ever more the livelong day,
Never work and never play,

Only stand and smile and pose
In the most expensive clothes.

And, these horrid words to prove,
Janet found she couldn't *move* . . .

In the window now she stands,
Holding out her waxen hands.
Other children as they pass
Drag their mothers to the glass:
'What a lovely coat and hat!
Look, Mamma! I *must* have that . . .'
And, these foolish words to hear,
Janet sheds a waxen tear.

Jan Struther

Jonathan

There was a boy called Jonathan
Who dreamt that he could fly.
He made himself some paper wings,
Determined he would try.
He stood upon the window sill,
Stretched out his arms and flew.
He got a bump upon his head,
A leg in plaster too.

Alison Winn

J

Poisonous Fruit

As Tommy and his sister Jane
Were walking down a shady lane,
They saw some berries, bright and red,
That hung around and overhead;

And soon the bough they bended down,
To make the scarlet fruit their own;
And part they ate, and part, in play,
They threw about, and flung away.

But long they had not been at home
Before poor Jane and little Tom
Were taken sick, and ill, to bed,
And since, I've heard, they both are dead.

Alas! Had Tommy understood
That fruit in lanes is seldom good,
He might have walked with little Jane
Again along the shady lane.

Elizabeth Turner

John and the Top Hat
A Tale of Tragedy

A fearful thing occurred to John.
He's put his father's topper on,
And all his efforts are in vain . . .
He cannot get it off again!
There's nothing one can do or say;
He's there, and there he'll have to stay.
They've done their best to mitigate
Johnny's uncomfortable fate.
They've cut two eye-holes for his eyes,
One for his mouth, a largeish size.
And in between (as you'd suppose)
Another hole to fit his nose.
So John can eat and see and smell,
And sing, and whistle pretty well.
He cannot wash . . . but to this boy
Washing was not a real joy . . .
And he can bear the deprivation
With commendable resignation.
  . . . The real tragedy is that
His father has no Sunday hat!

Edith F. B. MacAlister

The Cruel Boy

Jack Parker was a cruel boy,
For mischief was his sole employ;
And much it grieved his friends to find
His thoughts so wickedly inclined.

He thought it clever to deceive,
And often ramble without leave;
And every animal he met
He dearly loved to plague and fret.

But all such boys, unless they mend,
May come to an unhappy end,
Like Jack, who got a fractured skull,
Whilst bellowing at a furious bull.

Elizabeth Turner

The Boy Who Laughed at Santa Claus

In Baltimore there lived a boy.
He wasn't anybody's joy.
Although his name was Jabez Dawes,
His character was full of flaws.
In school he never led his classes,
He hid old ladies' reading glasses,
His mouth was open when he chewed,
And elbows to the table glued.

He stole the milk of hungry kittens,
And walked through doors marked *No admittance*.
He said he acted thus because
There wasn't any Santa Claus.
Another trick that tickled Jabez
Was crying 'Boo!' at little babies.
He brushed his teeth, they said in town,
Sideways instead of up and down.

Yet people pardoned every sin,
And viewed his antics with a grin,
Till they were told by Jabez Dawes,
'There isn't any Santa Claus!'
Deploring how he did behave,
His parents swiftly sought their grave.
They hurried through the portals pearly,
And Jabez left the funeral early.

Like whooping cough, from child to child,
He sped to spread the rumour wild:
'Sure as my name is Jabez Dawes
There isn't any Santa Claus!'
Slunk like a weasel or a marten
Through nursery and kindergarten,
Whispering low to every tot,
'There isn't any, no there's not!'

The children wept all Christmas Eve
And Jabez chortled up his sleeve.
No infant dared hang up his stocking
For fear of Jabez' ribald mocking.
He sprawled on his untidy bed,
Fresh malice dancing in his head,
When presently with scalp a-tingling,
Jabez heard a distant jingling;
He heard the crunch of sleigh and hoof
Crisply alighting on the roof.

What good to rise and bar the door?
A shower of soot was on the floor.
What was beheld by Jabez Dawes?
The fireplace full of Santa Claus!
Then Jabez fell upon his knees
With cries of 'Don't' and 'Pretty please'.
He howled, 'I don't know where you read it,
But anyhow, I never said it!'

'Jabez,' replied the angry saint,
'It isn't I, it's you that ain't.

Although there is a Santa Claus,
There isn't any Jabez Dawes!'
Said Jabez then with impudent vim,
'Oh, yes there is; and I am him!
Your magic don't scare me, it doesn't,' –
And suddenly he found he wasn't!

From grimy feet to grimy locks,
Jabez became a Jack-in-the-box,
An ugly toy with springs unsprung,
Forever sticking out his tongue.
The neighbours heard his mournful squeal;
They searched for him, but not with zeal.
No trace was found of Jabez Dawes,
Which led to thunderous applause,
And people drank a loving cup
And went and hung their stockings up.

All you who sneer at Santa Claus,
Beware the fate of Jabez Dawes,
The saucy boy who mocked the saint.
Doner and Blitzen licked off his paint.

Ogden Nash

The Story of Frozen James

What a charming boy was James!
Good at lessons, good at games,
Courteous to his aunts and others,
Patient with his younger brothers . . .

Yet this almost perfect lad
One unholy passion had:
He would think and talk and dream
All day long about ice-cream.

In the middle of the morning
First would come the tinkled warning;

Out he'd rush and gobble up
'Block' and 'cornet', 'brick' and 'cup'.
Then between his lunch and tea
He'd dispose of two or three,
And before the day was done
Manage yet another one.

Foolish child! This chilly diet
Caused his parents much disquiet.
'James,' they said with bated breath,
'Mark our words – you'll freeze to death.'

J

Parents' warnings (some have found)
Aren't so silly as they sound:
James, ignoring their advice,
One fine day was turned to ice.
What a lamentable plight!
Half was pink and half was white,
While where fingers should have been
Icicles were plainly seen.

'Will the wretched boy expire?
Quickly – we must light a fire!
Henry, fetch some sticks and straw . . . '
Just in time: his parents saw
James at last begin to thaw.

Now once more he's safe and warm,
Quite restored to human form:
But somehow he doesn't seem
Half so partial to ice-cream.

Jan Struther

There was a Little Girl

There was a little girl,
And she had a little curl
    Right in the middle of her forehead.
When she was good
She was very, very good
    And when she was bad she was horrid.

One day she went upstairs,
When her parents, unawares,
    In the kitchen were occupied with meals
And she stood upon her head
In her little trundle bed,
    And then began hooraying with her heels.

Her mother heard the noise,
And she thought it was the boys
    A-playing at a combat in the attic;
But when she climbed the stair,
And found Jemima there,
    She took and she did spank her most emphatic.

Anon

A Standing Order

When Mrs Keen commenced to teach
Her infant son the rules of speech,
  She started her instructions thus:
  'Pray never be ambiguous!

'Of any statement that you make,
Be sure there shall be no mistake,
  And be exact in what you mean –
  As I, you know, have always been.'

As Johnnie let his doubts appear
At that, his mother boxed his ear,
  And in a tone of stern command
  Right in the corner bade him *stand*.

She saw him to his place of doom,
Then rose and gently left the room;
  But on returning found instead
  Young Johnnie standing on his head.

Amazed at having to detect
A disobedience so direct,
  She cried, repeating the command:
  'I thought I told you, sir, to stand!'

J

Then, as she waited for a while,
A voice came off the velvet pile:
'You didn't say,' said Master John,
'Which end I was to stand upon.'

Hearing – with meaning misapplied –
Her careful lesson so decried,
His mother picked him up at that,
And whipped him soundly where he sat.

Laurence Housman

The Beet

'I will not wash my face I say;
I will not wash,' cried Jane, 'to-day.'
In vain mamma said, 'What disgrace!
To go with dirty hands and face!'
Jane only sulked and hung her head,
And so she crept away to bed.

Now when the pleasant morning broke
In bed the slovenly Jane awoke;
She woke but could not turn in bed,
Nor stretch herself, nor raise her head;
She was a beet with nose and eyes,
A beet of most enormous size.

And in the bed the beet leaves green
Instead of arms and legs were seen;
And then in came mamma and nurse;
They did not know her, which was worse,
But Jane could hear mamma; she said,
'Why, why! how came this beet in bed?'

And now, by two stout boys, away
They send the beet to town next day,
That all the people there may see
How large a beet can grow to be.
They put her in a window there,
Where every one can point and stare.

There the poor sloven sits and cries,
Till beet juice oozes from her eyes;
But ah! was such sight ever seen?
The beet juice tears have washed her clean;
And then, the strangest thing of all,
As fast and faster still they fall,

The beet tears melt her back once more
Into the child she was before.
She does not stay to wipe her eyes,
But home with eager feet she hies.
'Oh mother, mother dear,' cries she,
'Henceforth a cleaner child I'll be.'

Katherine Pyle

Cruel Joe

Joe was a very cruel boy;
To tease poor pussy was his joy.
He'd inch her tail till, scared, she fled,
Or in a stocking stuff her head.

But most of all he loved to spy
On window-panes a big blue fly.
He'd nimbly catch the buzzing thing;
Pull off a leg or else a wing.

One day, while playing with his toys,
He heard a curious humming noise.
He looked, and saw with eager eye
A new and interesting fly.

'Twas yellow, not, like others, blue;
Its waist was very slender too.
Thought Master Joe; 'It will be fun
To catch this pretty-coloured one!'

He seized it . . . but with skip and hop
He very quickly let it drop,
And screamed with pain and grief to find
How prickly was this fly behind.

When nurse came in to soothe his woe,
'Oh nurse!' he sobbed, 'it hurts me so;
A yellow fly that makes a hum
Has just sat down upon my thumb!'

Nurse viewed his thumb, and at the sight
Told cruel Joe it served him right.
'You thought you'd got a fly,' she said;
'You've been and caught a wasp instead!'

His tender thumb, all poulticed o'er,
Swelled twice the size it was before.
It ached and throbbed with might and main,
Till Joe grew dizzy with the pain.

At last he whimpered, sad and sore,
'I'll be a cruel boy no more;
But most of all will I be kind
To yellow flies with stings behind.'

W. Trego Webb

Silly Jackie

I wonder why poor Jackie cries?
The tears are streaming from his eyes.
  I really wonder what's the cause –
  He rolls his head and holds his jaws;
He keeps a flannel round his head,
But cannot even stay in bed.

Each moment, too, his screams get louder;
A toothbrush, with a little powder,
  Jack should have used both night and morning,
  And not have scoffed at every warning.
The toothache Jack now has is fearful,
And that is why he's sad and tearful.

He must be taken willy-nilly,
To get his teeth all out – the silly –
  He'll be a sight when home he comes
  With swollen cheeks and toothless gums.
The stupid boy, then, must be fed
On sago, porridge, milk, and bread;
  He won't get any pleasant treats,
  Not any biscuits, cakes nor sweets!

Isabel M. Carswell

Naughty Jemima

'Jemima!' said old Uncle Jimmie,
'As man and Christian 'tis my care
To tell you, what I'd often wished to,
Of all things evil do beware.
'Tis pleasant while the pleasures last,
But causes grief when they are past.'

'Indeed they're doomed,' said gentle Auntie,
'These wretched folks! I've known many such.
Therefore a child should wisely learn
To honour all old people much!
Now, good-night; it is late already,
Jemima, dear, pray and be steady!'

Jemima leaves the room. She sees
On Uncle's bed his night chemise.
So quickly with her needle goes,
And neck and arms together sews.

Then in a trice pops into bed,
And pulls the blankets o'er her head.

His bedroom now dear Uncle seeks
Yawning as he would crack his cheeks.

A final pinch of snuff he takes
Before his way to bed he takes.

His night-shirt then he tries to don
And struggles hard to get it on.

But though he tries with might and main
Yet all his efforts are in vain.

'I think that wonders ne'er will cease,'
Says Uncle, struggling with chemise.

He's working hard with main and might,
When ah! alas! Down goes the light!

His wrath increases more and more,
Snuff-box and watch fall on the floor.

His wrath explodes, great noise he makes,
And stumbling, all the china breaks.

The aunt comes in, and now is seen
Rags where a night-shirt once had been.

O wicked, naughty, graceless Miss,
How could you do a thing like this?

Willi Busch

Slovenly Kate

Oh, fie on Kate! untidy girl,
With dirty face, hair out of curl,
Who soils each dress, however neat,
First with the pudding, then with meat.
More like a little pig is she,
Than what a tidy girl should be!

Quite tired, at length, of all this waste,
One day Mama runs down in haste,
And brings three piggies straight upstairs
And round the table sets their chairs;
And Kate must needs e'en sit and dine,
Not with her playmates, but with swine!
And, truth to say, less clean was she,
Than either of the piggies three,
Who with good manners eat their meal,
While down Kate's cheeks the tear-drops steal.

The children laugh, when Kate they see,
In such unusual company.

Georg Glassbrenner

Getting Ready for School

Kate, Kate,
I know you'll be late!
Here is your satchel and here is your slate.
Don't go like that, Child, your hair's in a state –
Kate! Kate! Kate!

Kate, Kate,
It's twenty to nine,
Take your umbrella, it may not be fine.
Oh, what a hanky - you'd better take mine –
Kate! Kate! Kate!

Kate, Kate,
You haven't your fare!
Here are your sandwiches on the hall chair.
What's that? - your hockey stick - where darling where?
Kate! Kate! Kate!

Kate, Kate,
Your gym shoes are here,
Won't you be needing your pencil-box, dear?
Try to speak slower, love, Mother can't hear –
Kate! Kate! Kate!

Kate, Kate,
You'd better not wait,
The two little Smith girls have just passed the gate.
Hurry up, darling, I know you'll be late –
Kate! Kate! Kate!

Caryl Brahms

Kenneth
Who was too fond of bubble-gum
and met an untimely end

The chief defect of Kenneth Plumb
Was chewing too much bubble-gum.
He chewed away with all his might,
Morning, evening, noon and night.
Even (oh, it makes you weep)
Blowing bubbles in his sleep.

He simply couldn't get enough!
His face was covered with the stuff.
As for his teeth – oh, what a sight!
It was a wonder he could bite.
His loving mother and his dad
Both remonstrated with the lad.
Ken repaid them for the trouble
By blowing yet another bubble.

'Twas no joke. It isn't funny
Spending all your pocket money
On the day's supply of gum –
Sometimes Kenny felt quite glum.
As he grew, so did his need –
There seemed no limit to his greed:
At ten he often put away
Ninety-seven packs a day.

Then at last he went too far –
Sitting in his father's car,
Stuffing gum without a pause,
Found that he had jammed his jaws.
He nudged his dad and pointed to
The mouthful that he couldn't chew.
'Well, spit it out if you can't chew it!'
Ken shook his head. He couldn't do it.
Before long he began to groan –
The gum was solid as a stone.
Dad took him to a builder's yard;
They couldn't help. It was too hard.

They called a doctor and he said,
'This silly boy will soon be dead.
His mouth's so full of bubble-gum
No nourishment can reach his tum.'

Remember Ken and please do not
Go buying too much you-know-what.

Wendy Cope

Baby Kate

Darling little Baby Kate
Poured her broth on father's pate.
Father hollered: 'Hey, you goop!
That's my noodle in your soup!'

Joseph S. Newman

L

I shan't forget that little villain, L,
Who plagued me for a year in class 4C.
She used to take delight in raising hell.

Her name I won't reveal – it's just as well
To hide the dreadful child's identity.
I shan't forget that little villain, L.

The fire alarm went off – she rang the bell
After she locked me in the lavatory.
She used to take delight in raising hell.

The day we went pond-dipping, in she fell!
She couldn't swim, though I could, luckily
I shan't forget that little villain, L.

She let the gerbils out – they ran pell-mell.
Miss Pringle ended up in casualty.
She used to take delight in raising hell.

Although she was a problem, truth to tell,
I missed her when she ran away to sea.
I shan't forget that little villain, L.
She used to take delight in raising hell.

Sue Cowling

Lazy Lawrence

Lazy Lawrence loves his bed,
Lies there like a sleepy-head.

When he's called he gives a snore,
Turns and goes to sleep once more.

Home to dinner he will crawl,
Like a fat snail up a wall.

When he gets a holiday
He's too lazy, far, to play:

Cricket, football, all are one,
Lazy Lawrence cannot run.

Other boys ten sums can do
In the time that he does two.

Be a man some day? . . . Oh, no!
He's too lazy, far, to grow!

Clifton Bingham

Psychological Prediction

I think little Louie will turn out a crook. He
Puts on rubber gloves when stealing a cookie.

Virginia Brasier

Lazy Lou

Lazy Lou, Lazy Lou,
What's the matter, child, with you?
Can't you work, can't you play?
Can't you tuck your hair away?
If I were you, my Lazy Lou,
I'd change my ways, that's what I'd do.

Mary Mapes Dodge

Naughty Lizzy, the Greedy Girl

A little greedy tickle tooth,
Was Lizzy from her earliest youth;
Whate'er Ma hides, she's sure to find:
Preserves and jams of every kind,
Creams, custards, cakes must she hunt up,
Take here a bit and there a sup;
Into a jar now see she prys,
Filled with sweet stuff for killing flies:
She thinks 'tis syrup: oh, how nice!
Dip goes her finger in a trice!
She sucks it well between her lips,
Then in again she dips and dips.

But mark what ills in sweets lie hid,
When meant of flies a shelf to rid!
The syrup Lizzy thought a treat,
Rank poison held, altho' so sweet,
That such smart twinges made her feel,
You might from far have heard her squeal.
And nasty physic must she take,
For life itself was now at stake.

Soon after, when her birthday came,
She could not join in romp or game;
No children's feast could she partake . . .
She felt too sick to touch a cake:
No little friends to wish her joy,
No pretty gift of doll or toy!
For book, walk, play alike unfit,
Must Lizzy in her arm-chair sit.

Julius Baehr

The Chatterbox

From morning till night it was Lucy's delight
  To chatter and talk without stopping:
There was not a day but she rattled away,
  Like water for ever a-dropping.

No matter at all if the subjects were small,
  Or not worth the trouble of saying,
'Twas equal to her, she would talking prefer
  To working, or reading, or playing.

You'll think now, perhaps, that there would have been gaps,
  If she had not been wonderful clever:
That her sense was so great, and so witty her pate,
  It would be forthcoming for ever;

But that's quite absurd, for, have you not heard
  That much tongue and few brains are connected?
That they are supposed to think least who talk most,
  And their wisdom is always suspected?

While Lucy was young, had she bridled her tongue,
  With a little good sense and exertion,
Who knows, but she might now have been our delight,
  Instead of our jest and aversion?

Ann Taylor

Two Naughty Mabels

When guests were present, dear little Mabel
Climbed right up on the dinner-table
And naughtily stood upon her head!
'I wouldn't do that, dear,' Mamma said.

Carolyn Wells

Mabel, Mabel,
Are you able
To take your Elbows
Off the table . . . ?

Anon

Matilda

Matilda got her stockings wet,
And the result was, I regret,
Because she wouldn't change when told,
Matilda caught a dreadful cold.
Matilda sniffed and snuffled and sneezed,
Matilda choked and croaked and wheezed,
And the doctor came, and the doctor said
Matilda was to go to bed.
He sent her lozenges and lotions,
Some to be taken straight away,
And others three times every day,
With iodine to paint her skin,
And embrocation to rub in:
In fact, you might almost have filled a
Cart with the things he sent Matilda.
And yet Matilda, if you please,
Disliked the doctor's remedies.
Oh dear! there was a dreadful scene
Each time Matilda took quinine:
Matilda's yells came fast and faster
When they put on a mustard plaster:
Matilda's screams were even louder
When she was given Gregory's powder,
And it took half an hour's toil
To make her swallow castor oil.
I have known other painful cases,
But never seen such awful faces

As those that young Matilda made
On every visit the doctor paid.
What can you do with so self-willed a
Person as the girl Matilda?

★　　★　　★　　★

The other day I had a letter
To say Matilda was no better;
And from the way that she's behaving
Matilda doesn't seem worth saving.
Unless Matilda mends her ways
Upon the tombstone that they raise
Will be the words: 'Here lies Matilda.
Nothing but naughty temper killed her.'

F. Gwynne Evans

Indifference

When Grandmamma fell off the boat,
And couldn't swim (and wouldn't float),
Matilda just stood by and smiled.
I almost could have slapped the child.

Harry Graham

Maria and the Scissors

It chanced, one day, Maria found
A pair of scissors on the ground.
She seized them in an eager grip,
And looked around for things to snip.
Into the nursery first she ran,
And there her wild career began.
– For nurse, who would, of course, have checked it,
Had left the nursery unprotected –
She cut the curtains into strips,
Reduced the picture-books to snips;
She cut her little sister's hair,
Cut up the helpless Teddy-bear!

From room to room in haste she slipped,
And everything she saw, she snipped.
Carpets and counterpanes and sheets,
Even the cushions on the seats.
She cut the daily paper, and
Her father's magazine, the *Strand*;
And the umbrellas in the hall,
She clipped the covers from them all.

Into the garden next she went,
On her destructive mission bent.
She spent two busy, happy hours,
In cutting down her father's flowers.
Snip! went each Canterbury bell,
As from the parent stem it fell.

Snap! went the tulips, and each head
Fell, plop! upon the garden bed.
Snip! down went irises and stocks,
Carnations, lilies, roses, phlox!
Snap! down the stately sunflowers fall,
The scissors massacred them all.

Next, to the melon-frames she ran,
And devastation there began.
The gardener (a sleepy-head!)
Was dozing in the potting-shed,
And only wakened from his slumber
Just as she cut the last cucumber!
He woke too late to save (alas!)
The melons growing under glass.
And when, protesting, he appeared
Maria clipped his shaggy beard!

In grief and rage, the gardener-man
To tell Maria's father ran,
And left Maria at her ease
To cut the apples from the trees.
She gaily snipped off every peach
That hung within convenient reach.
She also clipped away some lots
Of promising young apricots.
Apples and cherries, plums as well,
And pears in myriads round her fell.
She sought the rows of early peas,
And cut down every one of these;
She cut the sprouts and curly-greens,
Leeks, marrows, cauliflowers, and beans!

Just then, her furious father came,
To interrupt Maria's game;
And he was cross, as you'd expect,
To see the place completely wrecked.
He saw the peaches strew the path,
A sight which woke still deeper wrath;
He gave a sort of growl – a gasp –
No words his rage would let him utter,
He snatched the scissors from her grasp,
And into seven pieces cut her!

Maria, now in fragments hewed,
Her wickedness most deeply rued.
Her father, too, was soon regretful
That he had been so cross and fretful.

Said he: 'I know what I will do!
I'll mend you up again with glue.'
To fetch the glue-pot, off he went,
And a most sticky hour he spent.

But – by some strange mischance, alack! –
(For mending he had little knack!)
He put her head on front to back!
And by the time he noticed, why,
It was too late, the glue was dry.

At first, Maria being mended,
Thought that her troubles all were ended.
But all too soon, she was awake
Unto her father's dire mistake.
Up to the house she backwards went,
A method inconvenient.
And sat down at the dinner-table
To eat as well as she was able.
But how it made her spirit droop
To find her pigtails in the soup!

Tears in her eyes began to glisten;
Her father said: 'Maria, listen!
All your discomfort and distress
Are caused by your own wickedness.
In future, scissorses eschew.
Meantime, to show I pardon you,
I'll melt you down this very day,
And glue your head the proper way.'

Edith F. B. MacAlister

Maria and the Inks

Maria was a wicked minx,
  With mischief always in her head.
She filled the milk-jug up with inks
  (Two kinds: the blue-black and the red).

With fury loud her father roared,
  When in his tea, that afternoon,
The mixture horrible was poured!
  He guessed the perpetrator soon.

'Abominable child!' he said,
  'I'll punish you for acting so!'
He seized Maria by the head
  And shook her fiercely to and fro.

In vain she tried away to slip,
  In vain she strove to twist and squirm,
He held her with a mighty grip,
  He held her very tight and firm.

What did he do then, do you think?
  Regardless of his daughter's shrieks,
He poured upon her head the ink
  Till she was red and black in streaks.

Edith F. B. MacAlister

Mary-Jane and Emily
Whose viewing habits came unstuck

I wonder if you've been to tea
With Mary-Jane and Emily,
Twin sisters both with golden curls,
The prettiest of little girls?

They're similar in many ways –
Not least in how their tempers blaze.
At tea-time, far from eating food,
The twins are resolutely glued
To television, when they fight
For what they're going to watch that night.
They never ever can agree
Upon which programme they will see.

They pull each other's hair about
And scratch and kick and sulk and pout.
Then one day, Emily let fly –
She hit her sister in the eye
Because she wanted 'Tom and Jerry'.
Gracious! Her vocabulary!
Mary-Jane picked up the jelly,
Missed her sister, hit the telly.
SPLAT! It landed on the screen.
(A pity. It was tangerine.)
Unfortunately, some of it
Ran down inside a tiny slit

And there coagulated, which
Jammed up the programme-channel switch.
The telly stayed for ever more
Immovably on Channel Four.

The sisters went to see their Mum.
'Please ask the engineer to come!'

He came, he saw, and then enquired.
'I s'pose you know this thing is hired?
You can't throw jelly at a box!
At least, it's most unorthodox.'
A word that made the sisters gasp.
(Its meaning's *still* beyond their grasp.)
The man was really most irate
And said, 'I'm going to confiscate
The television set right now –
This sort of thing we can't allow.'
And there and then, without delay,
He took the wretched thing away.

Poor Emily and Mary-Jane
Have never had a fight again.
They have to *talk* and *read* instead,
And go *much* earlier to bed.

The moral here is plain to see:
Don't watch the box while having tea.

Jeremy Nicholas

Meddlesome Matty

One ugly trick has often spoiled
   The sweetest and the best;
Matilda, though a pleasant child,
   One ugly trick possessed,
Which, like a cloud before the skies,
Hid all her better qualities.

Sometimes she'd lift the tea-pot lid,
   To peep at what was in it;
Or tilt the kettle, if you did
   But turn your back a minute.
In vain you told her not to touch,
Her trick of meddling grew so much.

Her grandmamma went out one day,
   And by mistake she laid
Her spectacles and snuff-box gay
   Too near the little maid;
'Ah! Well,' thought she, 'I'll try them on,
As soon as grandmamma is gone.'

Forthwith she placed upon her nose
   The glasses large and wide;
And looking round, as I suppose,
   The snuff-box too she spied;
'Oh! What a pretty box is that;
I'll open it,' said little Matt.

'I know that grandmamma would say,
   "Don't meddle with it, dear";
But then, she's far enough away,
   And no one else is near;
Besides, what can there be amiss
In opening such a box as this?'

So thumb and finger went to work
   To move the stubborn lid,
And presently a mighty jerk
   The mighty mischief did;
For all at once, ah! Woeful case,
The snuff came puffing in her face.

Poor eyes, and nose, and mouth, beside,
   A dismal sight presented;
In vain, as bitterly she cried,
   Her folly she repented.
In vain she ran about for ease;
She could do nothing now but sneeeze.

She dashed the spectacles away,
  To wipe her tingling eyes,
And as in twenty bits they lay,
  Her grandmamma she spies
'Heyday! And what's the matter now?'
Says grandmamma with lifted brow.

Matilda, smarting with the pain,
  And tingling still, and sore,
Made many a promise to refrain
  From meddling evermore.
And 'tis a fact, as I have heard,
She ever since has kept her word.

Ann Taylor

False Alarms

One day little Mary most loudly did call,
   'Mamma! O mamma, pray come here,
A fall I have had, oh! a very sad fall.'
   Mamma ran in haste and in fear.
Then Mary jumped up, and she laughed in great glee,
   And cried, 'Why, how fast you can run!
No harm has befall'n, I assure you, to me,
   My screaming was only in fun.'

Her mother was busy at work the next day,
   She heard from without a loud cry:
'The great Dog has got me! O help me! O pray!
   He tears me, he bites me, I die!'
Mamma, all in terror, quick to the court flew,
   And there little Mary she found;
Who, laughing, said, 'Madam, pray how do you do?'
   And curtseyed quite down to the ground.

That night little Mary was some time in bed,
   When cries and loud shrieking were heard:
'I'm on fire, O mamma! O come up, or I'm dead!'
   Mamma she believed not a word.
'Sleep, sleep, naughty child,' she called out from below,
   'How often have I been deceived!
You are telling a story, you very well know:
   Go to sleep, for you can't be believed.'

Yet still the child screamed: now the house filled with smoke:
  That fire is above, Jane declares:
Alas! Mary's words they soon found were no joke,
  When ev'ry one hastened up-stairs.
All burnt and all seamed is her once pretty face,
  And terribly marked are her arms,
Her features all scarred, leave a lasting disgrace,
  For giving mamma false alarms.

Adelaide O'Keeffe

Nina

Wee, experimental Nina
Dropped her mother's Dresden china
From a seventh-story casement,
Smashing, crashing to the basement.
Nina, somewhat apprehensive,
Said: 'This china is expensive,
Yet it proves by demonstration
Newton's law of gravitation.'

Wallace Irwin

Headstrong Nancy

Miss Nancy was a headstrong child;
And, let Mama say what she would,
She never listened nor was good,
But stamped and raved like one half wild,
Nor minded aught that she was bid,
And all her little playmates chid.

Now, Nancy she had dollies three,
And pretty ones, as you may see!
Who stood one night before her bed,
And, with uplifted fingers, said:
'Beware! Take care!
Your temper mend!
Or, naughty Nan
Shall, like a man,
A moustache wear;
And we will bend
Our steps afar
And go where better children are!'

But headstrong Nan their warning spurned;
And so, next night, the dolls returned
And o'er her lip, in frolic whim,
They fastened on a moustache grim,
Which gave her just as fierce an air
As any bandit bold might wear;

And then they laughed: 'Ho ho! ho ho!
We told you so
You naughty Nan!
Take off the moustache if you can!'

And then, Nan's tears and rage despite,
All three took flight,
And went afar,
Where better children are.

Now think, next morn, how Nan's ashamed,
And how she fears, Mama will scold,
And how she feels she must be blamed,
Soon as the secret dire is told.

Oh! what a bother!
Father, mother,
Aunt and cousins
By the dozens,
Call her 'Whiskered Nan!'
And haste as fast as haste they can,
And leave the town, to go afar,
To seek where better children are!

And when away they all had gone,
Unruly Nan was quite alone;
And, let her roar, and cry her fill,
A moustache can't be doffed at will;
So, though for grief her hands she wrung,
It ever after to her clung.

Georg Glassbrenner

Nancy

Nancy running in her nightgown
  Has no slippers has no socks
Running past the lighted houses
  Down to Peterphilly Rocks

Mother lights the front door lantern
  Father wrings and shakes his hands
Nancy running in her nightgown
  Down to Peterphilly sands

Moonlight shines on roofs and chimneys
  Moonlight shines on wheat and hay
Moonlight shines on deep bright water
  Down in Peterphilly Bay

Nancy running in her nightgown
  Has no slippers has no socks
Nancy running like a phantom
  Back from Peterphilly Rocks

Cara Lockhart Smith

What's a Pin?

'What's a pin?
  Mamma has plenty;
If I ask
  She'll give me twenty.
There, Nurse, hold your horrid din . . .
All this fuss about a pin.'

Saucy Ned
  Mamma has petted;
More he had
  The more he fretted;
And when spoken to by Nurse,
Sulked, and made the matter worse.

Nurse had said,
  A crumb untasted
Flung away
  Was surely wasted;
And a single pin when lost
Every hour, would money cost.

Little thought
  Ned on the morrow
That same pin
  Would cause him sorrow,
Or he ne'er had in his haste
Thrown away that pin in waste.

Next day Ned,
   Down in a corner,
Went to play
   At Jacky Horner.
When he gave a sudden cry
And to Nurse's lap did fly.

'Nurse, oh! Nurse!'
   He cried demented,
While with pain
   He nearly fainted;
'Take it out, oh! do, I beg;
See, it's sticking in my leg!'

In his leg
   The pin was sticking
And he had
   A painful pricking;
But he never any more
Threw a pin upon the floor.

Matthias Barr

Natasha Green

Natasha Green
Natasha Green
stuck her head in a washing machine

Washing machine
Washing machine
round and round Natasha Green

Natasha Green
Natasha Green
cleanest girl I've ever seen

Ever seen
Ever seen
a girl with her head in a washing machine?

Washing machine
Washing machine
last home of Natasha Green

Natasha Green
Natasha Green
washed away in a white machine

White machine
White machine
soaped to death Natasha Green

Natasha Green
Natasha Green
cleanest ghost I've ever seen!

MORAL:

Washing machines are for knickers and blouses
Washing machines are for jumpers and trousers
Keep your head out of the washing machine
or you'll end up as spotless as little Miss Green.

Ian McMillan

Mind The Gap!

Oliver was a doubting chap
Who heard the warning, MIND THE GAP!
And answered 'you're a silly sap!'
At Piccadilly station.

He slithered off his Mother's lap,
As soon as he heard MIND THE GAP!
Laughing: 'Don't get in a flap!'
At Piccadilly Station.

His mother tried to pull him back.
Too late! He'd tumbled down the crack
Leaving her his anorak
At Piccadilly Station.

So, children, stay on Mother's lap
Whenever you hear MIND THE GAP!
Or you will have a dire mishap,
Like Oliver, that doubting chap
At Piccadilly Station.

Anne Harvey

The Night Wanderer

When other children were asleep
Our Oswald down the stairs would creep
And to the fields he'd steal away,
Quite slyly by himself to play.
Sometimes he took the powder-horn,
And with the powder burnt the corn;

Sometimes he hid behind a tree,
And rushing out quite suddenly,
Would make a loud and fearful cry,
And frighten all the passers-by.
Indeed, it was his chief delight
To run away from home at night.
His parents shook their heads, and said,
'Oh! Oswald stay at home in bed,
For if you out at night do roam
A bat you surely will become.'

But all their talking was in vain;
Still Oswald would go out again.
But, oh! Just as his friends had said,
One night, as round the fields he sped,
Upon him came a wondrous change;
'Ah, me!' he cried, 'How very strange
I feel that I've become so small,
And now I cannot walk at all.

I put my hands up to my head,
But find a bat's face in its stead;
And now my hands are gone.
Oh, dear!
Instead of arms what have I here?

Such very, very curious things.
Why! Can they be? Oh, yes, they're wings.
Alas! Alas! What shall I do?
My parents' words are coming true.
An ugly bat I have become.
And never more shall I go home.'

Oh! Yes, my dears, it was too true;
An ugly bat away he flew;
His parents' tears streamed down like rain;
They never saw their child again.

Anon

The Story of Foolish Philip

Philip, when he walked to school
Bore in mind his mother's rule:
'When you wish to cross the street
Please be cautious and discreet.
In your purpose do not weaken . . .
Look for the Belisha beacon
Which with cheerful orange face
Smiles at every crossing-place
In between those studs of steel
You may safely set your heel,
While the traffic's raging tide
Stands respectfully aside;
(Drivers take especial care
Not to kill pedestrians there).'

P

All went well, until one day
Philip spied across the way
In the window of a shop
A delicious lollipop.
Straightway from his greedy head
All his mother's warnings fled:
Out he dashed with smile seraphic
Right into the thickest traffic . . .
What a dreadful scene it makes!
Skidding wheels and squealing brakes,
Hooting horns and tingling bells,
Women's shrieks and drivers' yells . . .
Vain, alas! The noise and fuss . . .
Philip lay beneath a bus.

Foolish boy! He was not dead,
But with sore and bandaged head
Ten long weeks he spent in bed;
And his mother made him say
Four-and-twenty times a day:

'I should not have had this pain
If I'd used a traffic lane.'

Jan Struther

The Story of Patrick in London

When Patrick went to London Town
To stay with Aunt Matilda Brown
He promised faithfully to do
Exactly what she told him to.
'Or else,' (his mother said), 'it's plain
You won't be asked to stay again.'
For several days young Patrick did
Most carefully as he was bid.
He brushed his hair and blew his nose
And folded up his underclothes
And washed his hands and wiped his feet
And walked sedately in the street . . .
In fact, he was so meek and mild
He seemed to her the Perfect Child;
And in return she tried to grant
His wishes like a Model Aunt.

They saw the Tower and the Zoo,
The Marble Arch, the Horse Guards too,
And that ingenious waxwork show
Designed by Madame M. Tussaud.
He much admired the Serpentine;
The Changing of the Guard was fine . . .
And all went well until they found
Themselves upon the Underground.

See! Aunt Matilda now prepares
To step upon the moving stairs.
She takes her little nephew's hand;
Upon the right they duly stand,
And off they go . . . but 'Hah!' cries Pat,
'I know a trick worth two of that!'
Astride the hand-rail down he flies
Before his aunt's astonished eyes.

'Come back!' she screams. 'You wicked boy!'
'All right, I will!' shouts Pat with joy;
Then up the other stair he nips
While Aunt Matilda downward slips;
And as she rises on his trail
He flashes past her down the rail.

So down and up and up and down
Go Pat and Aunt Matilda Brown,
Until she cries in sheer despair,
'Official! Stop the moving stair!'

Thus ends at last her breathless chase.
Poor Pat's sent home in deep disgrace,
And never more is asked to stay
In London for a holiday.

Jan Struther

151

Fretful Phoebe

Phoebe was a fretful child,
Nothing pleased her very long;
Half her pretty toys were spoiled,
Something always being wrong.

Books and pictures bought for her
Was but money thrown away;
Nurse declared they often were
Lost or torn in half a day!

If all Phoebes were the same,
We should shun their very sight,
But it sounds a pretty name
When we think of Phoebe Wright.

Elizabeth Turner

P

Penelope Pull-Rope

Penelope was wild and bold,
And though a girl of five years old,
She seldom did as she was told.

One special trick she had; 'twas this:
She reckoned it the height of bliss
To steal upstairs (the naughty miss!)

Pull any bell-rope that she found,
Then listen for the tinkling sound
And laugh when Nurse and Papa frowned.

One day within the bathroom door
She crept, a spot unsearched before,
Intent to spy one bell-rope more.

Above the door she smiled to see
A little cord that dangled free
'I'll pull it,' said Penelope.

So in the bath she climbed apace,
Then jerked the string, and oh! all trace
Of smiling vanished from her face,

For now, instead of tinkling bell
Down on her head (she pulled so well!)
A roaring flood of water fell.

Lamenting loud she ran below;
And everybody begged to know
Why she was drenched from top to toe.

With shaking limbs and aching head
They put her supper-less to bed;
And then her Nurse and Parents said:

'We trust you're sick as sick can be
Of pulling any rope you see.'
'I am,' said poor Penelope.

W. Trego Webb

Peter

I'm not sitting next to Peter
For he's such a messy eater,
And although he's my own brother,
Can't we swap him for another?
(For I'd much prefer a sibling
Who is not forever dribbling.)

Colin West

The Result of Heedlessness

Behold that speechless, aged Dame,
Who totters on the Arm
Of Thomas Brown, his sturdy Frame
Supporting her from Harm.

Sad is the Tale that I must tell,
The cause that struck her Dumb,
For to the Shock which her befell
She nearly did succumb.

Her Nephew Paul a little Mouse
Within the Barn had caught,
And in his Pocket to the House
The tiny Creature brought.

How wrong was Paul, for with Dismay
His Aunt a Rodent viewed,
How wickedly did he repay
Her kindness oft renewed.

The Work Box on the Table stood,
He quickly rais'd the Lid,
And 'mongst the Silks it did include
The Mouse securely hid.

She oped the Box, her Pins to seek,
Out sprang the nimble Mouse,
Oh Mercy! what a dreadful Shriek
Resounded through the House.

'Twas her last Cry, for ne'er again
Aunt Fanny's Voice was heard:
Depriv'd was she, by Shock and Pain,
Of Power to speak a Word.

Paul's Penitence was no avail,
The horrid Deed was done,
Though Good might through his Life prevail,
With Wrong it was begun.

How dread to think the Innocent
Must suffer for his Crime:
Mark how each Fault, though we repent,
Bears Consequence through Time.

Violet Jacob

Philip Never-Go-To-Bed

A snug and comfortable cot
Had Philip, but it pleased him not,
    And many a time he said
As twilight came, 'When I am old
And need not do as I am told,
    I'll never go to bed.'

One winter evening, when the time
Was near for seven o'clock to chime,
    The hour of his repose,
Oh, such a clever plan he tried!
'I'll run away,' thought he, 'and hide
    Myself where no-one knows.'

It chanced no servant was about,
His tender parents both were out,
    His nurse had left the room;
So, softly he unclosed the door,
And . . . what he'd never done before . . .
    Crept out into the gloom.

Soon after nurse returned, and took
A light and sought in every nook
   For Philip high and low.
His parents, vainly searching, passed
Through all the rooms, till tired at last
   They all to bed did go.

The morning dawned, and no-one stirred,
When all at once a sound was heard,
   A lamentable cry,
That issued forth from underneath
A chest of drawers, through chattering teeth,
   'Oh, mother, where am I?'

'Twas Philip's voice; the naughty boy
Had crawled beneath the chest with joy
   At thinking there to keep
Secure from nurse and parents' eyes
When, very much to his surprise,
   He'd fallen fast asleep.

Up came the nurse and found him there,
Chilled through and through with mid-night air;
   And, coughing much, he said:
'Oh, nurse, I'll never treat you so
Again, but always punctual go
   At seven o'clock to bed!'

W. Trego Webb

Quarrelsome Queenie

See her with her angry face,
Is she not a sad disgrace?

Queenie Quarrelsome's her name.
Queenie, Queenie, fie for shame!

If it's not a game she knows,
Soon her face with anger glows;

Nobody with her will play,
From her they all run away.

Indoors, outdoors, 'tis the same,
Queenie Quarrelsome's her name.

Vexes brothers, sisters, nurse,
And her mother, which is worse!

There's but one thing to be done,
Find a cupboard, nice dark one,

Put her on the highest shelf . . .
Let her quarrel by herself!

Clifton Bingham

Two People

Two people live in Rosamund,
  And one is very nice;
The other is devoted
  To every kind of vice —

To walking where the puddles are,
  And eating far too quick,
And saying words she shouldn't know,
  And wanting spoons to lick.

Two people live in Rosamund,
  And one (I say it twice)
Is very nice *and* very good:
  The other's only nice.

E. V. Rieu

Nothing, That's What

'What ARE you doing, Rupert?'
There comes the same reply,
For Rupert answers, 'Nothing.'
And that's his daily cry.

'What are you DOING, Rupert?
Who broke the garden pot?'
But Rupert answers, 'Nothing.'
And nothing's not a lot.

Whenever people blame him
For doing such-and-such
Then Rupert's doing nothing,
Which isn't very much.

'WE want to SEE you, Rupert,
Who made this awful mess?'
But Rupert's doing nothing,
Well, Nothing more or less.

And so we have this problem
To puzzle anyone,
How Rupert's doing nothing,
Yet naughty things are done.

Max Fatchen

Reginald Roy

A restless and reckless and rollicking boy,
Just crammed full of mischief was Reginald Roy;
He sat on the tables, he jumped over chairs,
But what he liked best was to slide down the stairs.
Though his father and mother both lectured him daily,
Yet still he would slide down the bannisters gaily.

One day from the landing above he came swinging,
It was just at the moment that Mary was bringing
The soup in for dinner, and Reginald fell
Right over the stairs with a horrible yell.
  Into Mary he crashed,
  The soup-dish was smashed,
And his feet and his hands, and his arms and his knees
Were splashed with small pieces of carrots and peas,
  While parsley and leeks
  Bespattered his cheeks,

And there he lay moaning,
And sobbing and groaning,
With both his legs broken, and cuts on his ears?
(When his poor mother saw him she burst into tears!)

The doctor then bandaged his legs and his head,
And they carried him tenderly up to his bed,
And he lay very ill
For a long time, until
He could hobble about, oh, so slowly with crutches.
He would think it a treat
To get using his feet
Though he once slid about like a monkey, for such is
Poor Reginald's fate
That he longs to be good when, alas, it's too late!
And this tale has a moral that no boy should lose,
Or he'll find himself standing in Reginald's shoes.

Isabel M. Carswell

Rebecca
Who slammed Doors for fun and
Perished Miserably

A Trick that everyone abhors
In Little Girls is slamming doors.
A Wealthy Banker's Little Daughter
Who lived in Palace Green, Bayswater
(By name Rebecca Offendort),
Was given to this Furious Sport.

She would deliberately go
And slam the door like Billy-Ho!
To make her uncle Jacob start.
She was not really bad at heart,
But only rather rude and wild;
She was an aggravating child.

It happened that a Marble Bust
Of Abraham was standing just
Above the Door this little Lamb
Had carefully prepared to Slam,
And Down it came! It knocked her flat!
It laid her out! She looked like that!

Her Funeral Sermon (which was long
And followed by a Sacred Song)
Mentioned her Virtues, it is true,
But dwelt upon her Vices, too,
And showed the Dreadful End of One
Who goes and slams the Door for Fun.

Hilaire Belloc

Dirge for a Bad Boy

Richard has been sent to bed:
Let a solemn dirge be said.
Sent to bed before his time,
Sentenced for a nursery crime.
Draw down the blind in every room
And fill the dismal house with gloom.
Richard has been sent to bed:

Let a solemn dirge be said.
Tell the cat and Kitten they
Must cease from their unseemly play.
Stop the telephone from ringing;
Stop the Kettle from its singing.
And hark, is that the Hoover's hum?
Let the Hoover too be dumb.
Richard has been sent to bed:
Let a solemn dirge be said.

Turn off, turn off, the central heat,
And let the cold creep round our feet.
Put out the fire and let it die
Underneath the juicy pie,
That we may eat (if eat we must)
Cold apple and a colder crust.
Richard has been sent to bed;
Let a solemn dirge be said.

And when the time has come for all
To follow through the darkened hall,
Let every sound of mirth be banned –
Take each candle in his hand,
And winding up the stairway slow
In melancholy order go,
While this solemn dirge is said
For a poor sinner in his bed.

E. V. Rieu

Richard

A boy called Richard I once knew
Made aeroplanes of wood and glue.
Delighted when they were complete,
He wiped his hands upon his seat.
When Mother called, 'It's time for tea,'
He ate a large meal hungrily,
Politely asked to leave the table
And found in fact he wasn't able.

If you should see him, please don't stare,
He walks around glued to his chair.

Alison Winn

S

Prudent Little Ned

'My dear little Ned,'
His grandmamma said,
'I think I have cautioned you twice,
I hope you'll take heed,
I do, love, indeed,
And I'll beg you'll not venture on ice.

'Good skaters, I know,
On the ice often go
And also will others entice,
When there has not been frost
Two days at the most,
And when very thin is the ice.'

He went to the brook,
Resolved but to look,
And thought he could slide very nice,
And the slides were so long,
He knew 'twould be wrong,
So he did not then go on the ice.
He wisely behaved,
And his life thus was saved;
For Sam Headstrong (who ne'er took advice)
Went where it was thin.
Alas! he fell in:
He sank, and went under the ice.

Elizabeth Turner

Impetuous Samuel

Sam had spirits nought could check,
    And to-day, at breakfast, he
Broke his baby sister's neck,
    So he shan't have jam for tea!

Harry Graham

My Sister Sybil

Sipping soup, my sister Sybil
Seems inclined to drool and dribble.
If it wasn't for this foible
Meal-times would be more enjoyable!

Colin West

Miss Sophia

Miss Sophy, one fine sunny day,
Left her work and ran away;
When soon she reach'd the garden-gate,
Which finding lock'd, she would not wait,
But tried to climb and scramble o'er
A gate as high as any door.
But little girls should never climb,
And Sophy won't another time;
For when, upon the highest rail,
Her frock was caught upon a nail:
She lost her hold, and, sad to tell,
Was hurt and bruised – for down she fell.

Elizabeth Turner

Sulky Susan

Sulky Susan has no friends,
All alone her time she spends;

While the others romp and play,
She prefers to sulk all day.

Sulks because it isn't fine,
Sulks because the sun will shine:

Sulks to get up when it's light,
Sulks to go to bed at night.

Such an ugly, sulky face
Is a cloud upon the place;

All the cats and dogs, they say,
When they see it, run away!

Oh! her face is such a sight,
It's no wonder they take fright;

If you saw her coming, you
Would be very frightened, too!

Clifton Bingham

Sammy Sweet-Tooth

That greedy little fellow Sam,
His parents once had left alone . . .
But warned him well he should not cram
His throat with sweets while they were gone.

But scarcely had they both gone out,
When Sammy rummaged all about,
'Mongst pans and bottles in a trice,
In hopes of finding something nice.

A dish beside the oven stood . . .
This sure contains some dainty food!
He lifts the lid, and finds a cake
Of dough, well-kneaded, fit to bake.

Then straight his fingers in he dips,
And greedily he licks their tips;
And O! it tastes so very sweet,
He smacks his lips at such a treat.

A second piece he can't resist,
Nor will a third, he thinks, be missed,
And then three pieces lead to four;
For much will always crave for more.

He lingers, loth to leave his prize,
When lo! the yeast begins to rise,
And not within the dish alone ...
In Sammy's paunch it up has blown!

Now mark how bloated is his face,
And how his body swells apace!
And how he glares with goggle eyes,
To see his body such a size!

'Oh dear!' he roars, 'I'm like a drum!'
And when his mother home has come,
So big is grown her little son,
He cannot waddle ... much less run.

Still, like a bubble filled with air,
He swells enough to make one stare,
And should the worst come to the worst,
Tomorrow he will surely burst!

Georg Glassbrenner

Naughty Susan, the Fretful Child

While other children, blithe and gay,
In frolic sports would spend the day,
Cross Susan played not, out of spite,
For nought with her was ever right.
She ne'er enjoyed a tart or cake,
Nor in a toy would pleasure take . . .
And though she nothing really ailed
She always cried, or stormed, or railed.
In vain her mother used to say:
'Now, Susan, do not cry all day.'
The headstrong girl still gave not o'er,
But only wept and wept the more.

At length one day, so long she cried
That round her flowed the briny tide,
First ankle deep, then higher still
Rising began the room to fill.
Next knee-deep, then waist high the flood
Beyond high-water mark soon stood.

And as her tears still ceaseless flowed,
Across their flood you might have rowed:
But Susan lacking oar and boat,
Could neither stand, and scarcely float.
Thus 'mid the tears, her eyes that dim,
She floundered, all unused to swim,

And must have soon been drowned outright,
Had not her Ma, who saw her plight,
Now rescued her from out the wet,
And fished up Susan in a net.

Julius Baehr

Prying Little Tom

Prying little Tom
  Peeping in the pot;
Tell me, Tommy, come,
  What have you got?
Standing on your toes,
  Reaching over so?
I have burnt my nose;
  Oh! oh! oh!
Better had you gone to bed
  After lessons, as Ma said.

Matthias Barr

Little Thomas

Thomas was a little glutton
Who took four times beef or mutton,
Then undid a lower button
 And consumed plum-duff,
And when he could scarcely swallow
Asked if there was more to follow,
As he'd still a tiny hollow
 That he'd like to stuff.

He was told: 'You won't get thinner
While you will eat so much dinner;
If you don't take care, some inner
 Part of you will burst.'
He replied: 'What does it matter
Even if I do get fatter?
Put more pudding on my platter:
 Let it do its worst.'

Then one day, and little wonder,
There was a report like thunder:
Doors and windows flew asunder,
 And the cat had fits.
As his anxious friends foreboded,
Dangerously overloaded
Thomas had at length exploded,
 And was blown to bits.

His old nurse cried, much disgusted,
'There, just when I've swept and dusted,
Drat the boy! he's gone and busted,
    Making such a mess.'
While the painful task of peeling
Thomas off the walls and ceiling
Gave his family a feeling
    Of sincere distress.

When a boy, who so obese is,
Scatters into tiny pieces,
And the cause of his decease is
    Having overdined,
It is hard to send a version
Of the facts of his dispersion
To the papers for insertion
    Which will be refined.

Any sorrowing relation
Asked for an elucidation
Of the awful detonation
    Was obliged to say:
'Germans have not been to bomb us:
It was only little Thomas,
Who, alas! departed from us
    In that noisy way.'

F. Gwynne Evans

Untidy Tom

Tom was a most untidy boy,
Who took no care of book or toy;
Nor were his clothes e'er neatly laid
Beside him when he went to bed.

No, nothing in its place was found,
But all his things were strewn around;
His socks at random off he tossed,
As though he cared not both were lost.

Besides the stove was seen a shoe,
His trousers there were lying too;
The fellow shoe was near the door,
Flung with the coat upon the floor.

But, children, mark what happened next,
And think how sorely Tom was vexed!
At early morn his father rose
And dressed the dog up in his clothes!

He dressed him in the coat so warm,
And put a book beneath his arm;
While Tom was forced to stand and look,
Though in his shirt with cold he shook.

What think you next his father did?
Why, little Tom he straightway bid
With doggy thus to school to go,
That doggy might his learning show!

And Tom most foolish looked, I trow,
As forth he went amid the snow;
While proudly stalked the dog, you see,
As though he'd taken his degree!

Georg Glassbrenner

Envious Tom

Tom was to envious habits prone,
　　Another's joys would make him sad,
He valued nothing of his own,
　　But longed for all his sister had.

Their uncle once a visit paid,
　　When to them both he kindly said:
'I've brought two presents all alive,
　　And one to each I mean to give.

'Now see this cat so snowy white
　　With skin as soft as eiderdown;
And see this dog . . . he'll never bite . . .
　　Whose little snout wears spots of brown.
The cat, dear Jane's, the gift I make
To you . . . while Tom shall doggy take.'

So pleased is Jane on hearing this,
　　She thanked her uncle with a kiss;
But Tommy in a rage doth cry:
　　'I won't have doggy . . . no, not I;

T

So pussy will I take instead:'
  And up he jumps as soon as said;
Straight by the tail he seizes her,
  And roughly handles pussy's fur.

But Tom soon found he was no match
  For frightened Puss, began to scratch;
And with such rage his cheeks they tore,
  The blood ran trickling on the floor,

And much I wish that pussy's marks
  May Tommy to his senses bring.
Meanwhile the doggy stands and barks:
  'See! Envy is a nasty thing!'

Georg Glassbrenner

Tommy would not go to Bed

Young Tommy would not go to bed,
But sat watching TV instead,
    As he stayed up to stare
His face went all square
And aerials grew from his head.

Anon

A Folk Rhyme

Tom tied a kettle to the tail of a cat,
Jill put a stone in the blind man's hat,
Bob threw his grandmother down the stairs –
And they all grew up ugly, and nobody cares.

Anon

Tom's Bomb

There was a boy whose name was Tom,
Who made a high explosive bomb,
By mixing up some iodine
With sugar, flour and plasticine.
Then, to make it smell more queer,
He added Daddy's home-made beer.
He took it off to school one day,
And when they all went out to play,
He left it by the radiator.
As the heat was getting greater,
The mixture in the bomb grew thick
And very soon it seemed to tick.
Miss Knight came in and gazed with awe
To see the bomb upon the floor.
'Dear me,' she said, 'it is a bomb,
An object worth escaping from.'
She went to Mr Holliday
And said in tones that were not gay,
'Headmaster, this is not much fun;
There is a bomb in Classroom One.'
'Great snakes,' said he, and gave a cough
And said, 'I hope it won't go off.
But on the off-chance that it does,
I think we'd better call the fuzz.'
A policeman came and said, 'Oh God,
We need the bomb disposal squad,

Some firemen and a doctor too,
A helicopter and its crew,
And, since I'm shaking in the legs,
A pot of tea and hard-boiled eggs.'
A bomb disposal engineer
Said, with every sign of fear,
'I've not seen one like that before,'
And rushed out, screaming, through the door.
Everyone became more worried
Till Tom, who seemed to be unflurried,
Asked what was all the fuss about?
'I'll pick it up and take it out.'
He tipped the contents down the drain
And peace and quiet reigned again.
Tom just smiled and shook his head
And quietly to himself he said:
'Excitement's what these people seek.
I'll bring another one next week.'

David Hornsby

Tom and the Pins

From his toes up to his shins
    Tom stuck Grandpa full of pins;
Although Tom the fun enjoyed,
    Grandpapa was quite annoyed.

Anon

iveb

Twin Trouble

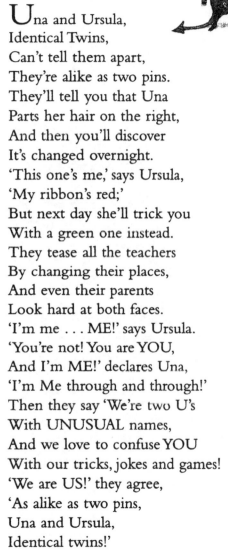

de'

Una and Ursula,
Identical Twins,
Can't tell them apart,
They're alike as two pins.
They'll tell you that Una
Parts her hair on the right,
And then you'll discover
It's changed overnight.
'This one's me,' says Ursula,
'My ribbon's red;'
But next day she'll trick you
With a green one instead.
They tease all the teachers
By changing their places,
And even their parents
Look hard at both faces.
'I'm me . . . ME!' says Ursula.
'You're not! You are YOU,
And I'm ME!' declares Una,
'I'm Me through and through!'
Then they say 'We're two U's
With UNUSUAL names,
And we love to confuse YOU
With our tricks, jokes and games!
'We are US!' they agree,
'As alike as two pins,
Una and Ursula,
Identical twins!'

Anne Harvey

Vain Victor

Victor was so very vain,
Oft he gave his mother pain;
'Oh!' she cried, 'what shall we do
With a peacock-boy like you?'
Vain of this and vain of that,
Of his Sunday clothes and hat,
Warned again, and yet again,
Still he went on being vain!

Soon a change came over him,
Both in feature and in limb;
He grew much too vain to speak,
Then came feathers, tail, and beak!

After this, so I have learned,
He into a peacock turned.
Boys and girls, take warning, do,
Lest you turn to peacocks too!

Clifton Bingham

Wicked Willie

Willie was a wicked boy,
Snubbed his poor old mother;
Willie was a dreadful boy,
Quarrelled with his brother;
Willie was a spiteful boy,
Often pinched his sister;
Once he gave her such a blow
Raised a great big blister!

Willie was a sulky boy,
Sadly plagued his cousins;
Often broke folks' window panes,
Throwing stones by dozens;
Often worried little girls,
Bullied smaller boys;
Often broke their biggest dolls,
Jumped upon their toys.

If he smelt a smoking tart,
Willie longed to steal it;
If he saw a pulpy peach,
Willie tried to peel it;
Could he reach a new plum-cake,
Greedy Willie picked it;
If he spied a pot of jam,
Dirty Willie licked it.

If he saw a poor old dog,
Wicked Willie whacked it;
If it had a spot of white,
Silly Willie blacked it;
If he saw a sleeping cat,
Horrid Willie kicked it;
If he caught a pretty moth,
Cruel Willie pricked it.

If his pony would not trot,
Angry Willie thrashed it;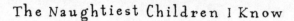
If he saw a clinging snail,
Thoughtless Willie smashed it;
If he found a sparrow's nest,
Unkind Willie hid it.
All the mischief ever done,
Folks knew Willie did it.

No one liked that horrid boy,
Can you wonder at it?
None who saw his ugly head
Ever tried to pat it.
No one took him for a ride –
Folks too gladly skipped him;
No one gave him bats or balls,
No one ever tipped him.

No one taught him how to skate,
Or to play at cricket;
No one helped him if he stuck
In a prickly thicket.
Oh no! for the boys all said
Willie loved to tease them,
And that if he had the chance,
Willie would not please them.

And they shunned him every one,
And they would not know him;
And their games and picture-books
They would never show him;
And their tops they would not spin,
If they saw him near them;
And they treated him with scorn,
Till he learnt to fear them.

They all left him to himself,
And he was so lonely;
But of course it was his fault,
Willie's own fault only.
If a boy's a wicked boy,
Shy of him folks fight then;
If it makes him dull and sad,
Why, it serves him right then!

Anon

Winifred Waters

Winifred Waters sat and sighed
  Under a weeping willow;
When she went to bed she cried,
  Wetting all her pillow;

Kept on crying night and day,
  Till her friends lost patience;
'What shall we do to stop her, pray?'
  So said her relations.

Send her to the sandy plains
  In the zone called torrid.
Send her where it never rains,
  Where the heat is horrid.

Mind that she has only flour
  For her daily feeding;
Let her have a page an hour
  Of the driest reading –

Navigation, logarithm,
  All that kind of knowledge –
Ancient pedigrees go with 'em
  From the Herald's College.

When the poor girl has endured
  Six months of this drying,
Winifred will come back cured,
  Let us hope, of crying.

William Brighty Rands

Whining Whinnie

Be the weather wet or fine,
Winifred can only whine;

Nothing's pleasant, nothing's right,
Morning, afternoon, or night!

Whines because the sun's too hot,
Whines though all she wants she's got.

Whines at school and whines at play,
Whines, indeed, through all the day!

She has dollies, quite a score,
Still she whines for just one more;

Whines to rise, to go to bed . . .
She is whining Winifred.

I believe if she had been
Born a Princess or a Queen,

She'd have whined all day to be
Just a girl like you or me!

Clifton Bingham

Prying Will

Will so delights to peep and pry,
That all about the house he goes,
Upstairs and down, from low to high,
And everywhere he pokes his nose.

Into the kitchen now he comes,
Where that same morn, with luscious plums,
Made into jam, and still quite hot . . .
The Cook had filled a giant pot.

Will must, of course, remove the lid
To see what treasures there lie hid,
When . . . lost his balance . . . up he trips,
And plump! head foremost in he slips.

His feet are seen above the rim,
But sure the pot has swallowed him!
And buried in its sweets he lies,
That fill his mouth and stop his cries!

But Cook now shrieks, though Will is dumb . . .
His startled parents quickly come,
And drag out Billy in a fright.
Oh, lack-a-day! Oh, what a sight!

Blue is his jacket, shirt and frill,
And blue inside and out is Bill!
  So blue, so blue,
  Through life he'll rue
The foolish prank that made him so;
For ne'er away the stain would go . . .

But blue face, neck and hands remained,
And thus the name of Prying Bill he gained!

Georg Glassbrenner

Careless Willie

Willie, with a thirst for gore,
Nailed his sister to the door.
Mother said, with humour quaint:
'Now, Willie dear, don't scratch the paint.'

Anon

Xcitable X

This small boy's name I dare not state
  If he his name should see
In print, it might arouse his great
  Xcitabilitee.
If he should here his portrait meet,
  He'd fly into a rage,
And clench his fist, and stamp his feet,
  And tear, right out, this page.
Though sorry afterwards he'd be,
  His temper we won't vex,
'Twould be too late when done, so we
  Will simply call him X.

Clifton Bingham

Yawning Yolande

From the time when morning dawns
Till her bed-time comes she yawns;
Yawns at breakfast and at tea,
Such a yawning girl is she.
'Shut your mouth!' her mother cries,
'Or you'll soon catch all the flies!'

One night, as she snoring slept
Mousie to her pillow crept,
Saw her big mouth open wide,
Very nearly stole inside.
If she doesn't mind, they say,
She will yawn too far some day,
Then through life she'll have to go
With her mouth wide open ... so!

Clifton Bingham

Zachary's Progress

Zachary liked pulling faces,
All day long he'd make grimaces,
And at school he'd taunt his teachers
With contortions of his features.

Sitting at his school desk smugly,
Once he pulled a face so ugly,
That he gave poor Miss McKenzie
Cause to fly into a frenzy:

Mouth wide open – how revolting!
Tongue protruding – how insulting!
Puffed-out cheeks and wrinkled forehead –
Zachary looked really horrid!

Thus it was the nasty creature
So provoked his gentle teacher,
That she, driven to distraction,
Took at once most drastic action.

Pelting him with books, she dented
Poor Zach's head till he repented,
And agreed that when at places
Such as school, he'd not pull faces.

Let us now praise Miss McKenzie,
She who flew into a frenzy,
And in just one scripture session,
Made a permanent impression.

Colin West

199

An Alphabet of Horrible Habits

 A is for Albert who makes lots of noise

 B is for Bertha who bullies the boys

 C is for Cuthbert who teases the cat

 D is for Dilys whose singing is flat

 E is for Enid who's never on time

 F is for Freddy who's covered in slime

 G is for Gilbert who never says thanks

 H is for Hannah who plans to rob banks

I is for Ivy who slams the front door

 J is for Jacob whose jokes are a bore

K is for Kenneth who won't wash his face

 L is for Lucy who cheats in a race

M is for Maurice who gobbles his food

 N is for Nora who runs about nude

O is for Olive who treads on your toes

 P is for Percy who *will* pick his nose

Q is for Queenie who won't tell the truth

R is for Rupert who's rather uncouth

 S is for Sibyl who bellows and bawls

T is for Thomas who scribbles on walls

U is for Una who fidgets too much

 V is for Victor who talks double Dutch

W is for Wilma who won't wipe her feet

X is for Xerxes who never is neat

Y is for Yorick who's vain as can be

 and Z is for Zoe who doesn't love me.

Colin West

Acknowledgements

The Author and publishers would like to thank the following people for giving permission to include in this anthology material which is their copyright. The publishers have made every effort to trace copyright holders. If we have inadvertently omitted to acknowledge anyone we should be most grateful if this could be brought to our attention for correction at the first opportunity.

JULIUS BAEHR (German 19th Century): 'Naughty Dan, the Deceitful Boy', 'Naughty Lizzy, the Greedy Girl' and 'Naughty Susan, the Fretful Child', from *Naughty Boys & Girls*. Translated by Mme Clara De Chatelain. Illustrated by Theodor Hosemann. (Addey & Co. 1852)

ZOË BARBER (b. 1985): 'Alice, who had a bad habit of throwing things', was winner of the Wycombe Abbey School Poetry Writing Competition under 12 section, printed by permission of the author.

GEORGE BARKER (1913-1991): 'My Sister Clarissa' from *To Aylsham Fair*, (Faber & Faber 1970) reprinted by permission of Faber.

MATTHIAS BARR (19th Century): 'Prying Little Tom' and 'What's a Pin?', from *Hours Of Sunshine*, (James Nisbet & Co 1869).

HILAIRE BELLOC (1870-1953): 'Rebecca' and 'Henry King', from *Cautionary Tales For Children*, (Duckworth & Co. 1907), reprinted by permission of the Peter Fraser & Dunlop Group Ltd.

MARY BELSON (sometimes ELLIOT) (1794-1870): 'The Busy Child', from *Simple Truths* (Wm Darton 1816).

CLIFTON BINGHAM (1859-1913): 'Dirty Dick', 'Envious Eliza', 'Fidgety Frank', 'Lazy Lawrence', 'Quarrelsome Queenie', 'Sulky Susan', 'Vain Victor', 'Whining Winnie,' 'Xcitable X' and 'Yawning Yolande' from *Six and Twenty Boys and Girls* (Blackie & Son 1902).

CARYL BRAHMS (1901-1982): 'Bad Boy Benjamin' from *Curiouser and Curiouser*, (Haverstock Ltd 1932). 'Getting Ready for School', printed in the *Evening Standard*, circa 1930, both are reprinted by permission of Ned Sherrin.

VIRGINIA BRASIER (American): 'Psychological Prediction', (Louis) printed in the *New Yorker* Magazine 1942.

Acknowledgements

SIMON BRETT (b. 1942): 'Ivor Brown', from *The Child-Owner's Handbook*, (Unwin 1983), reprinted by permission of the author.

WILLIAM BRIGHTY RANDS (1823-1882): 'Godfrey Gordon Gustavus Gore', 'Winifred Waters' and 'Shut the Door', from *Lilliput Lyrics* (1886)

GELETT BURGESS (American 1866-1951): 'Felicia Ropps', from *The Goops Anthology*.

WILLI BUSCH (German 19th Century): 'Naughty Jemima', translated from the German by John Maclush, (Ward, Lock & Tyler 1874).

ISABEL M. CARSWELL: 'Bad Belinda', 'Silly Jackie' and 'Reginald Roy', from *Marjory May*, (Gowans & Gray Ltd 1913).

WENDY COPE (b. 1945): 'Kenneth', from *Uncollected Poems* (1985), reprinted by permission of the author.

SUE COWLING: 'L', from *What is a Kumquat?* (Faber & Faber 1991), reprinted by permission of the author.

MARY MAPES DODGE (American 1831-1905): 'Lazy Lou', from *Rhymes & Jingles* (1904).

PEGGY DUNSTAN (New Zealand b. 1926): 'Porridge', from *In & Out the Windows*, (Hodder & Stoughton 1980), reprinted by permission of the author.

ELEANOR FARJEON (1881-1965): 'Griselda', from *The Children's Bells* (OUP 1957) reprinted by permission of Gervase Farjeon.

MAX FATCHEN (Australian b. 1920): 'Nothing, That's What', from *Wry Rhymes for Troublesome Times*, (Kestrel 1983) reprinted by permission of John Johnson Ltd.

ROY FULLER (1912-1991): 'Ermyntrude', from *The World Through the Window*, (Blackie 1989) reprinted by permission of John Fuller.

JIMMY GARTHWAITE (American): 'Little Arty', from *PUDDIN' an' PIE* (Harper & Row 1929).

GEORG ADOLF THEODOR GLASSBRENNER (German 19th Century): 'Screaming Annie', 'Charley the Story-Teller', 'Slovenly Kate', 'Headstrong Nancy', 'Sammy Sweet-Tooth', 'Envious Tom' and 'Untidy Tom' and 'Prying Will' from *A Laughter Book (Lachende Kinder)* translated by Mme De Chatelain, Illustrated by Theodor Hosemann (Cundall & Addey 1851).

ELIZABETH GODLEY: 'Extremely Naughty Children', from *Green Outside*, illustrated by Rex Whistler (Chatto & Windus 1931), reprinted by permission of Mary O'Connell, with thanks to The Right Hon. Lord Kilbracken.

HARRY GRAHAM (1874-1936): 'Inconsiderate Hannah' and 'Impetuous Samuel', from *Ruthless Rhymes For Heartless Homes* (Edward Arnold 1899). 'Indifference' and 'Quiet Fun', from *More Ruthless Rhymes* (Edward Arnold

Acknowledgements

1930). Reprinted by permission of the trustees of the estate of Virginia Thesiger, under the Copyright, Designs and Patent Act 1988, with thanks to Peter de Vic Carey of William Sturges Solicitors.

F. GWYNNE EVANS: 'Matilda' and 'Little Thomas', from *Puffin, Puma & Co*, (Macmillan & Co. 1929).

ANNE HARVEY (b. 1933): 'Isaac Beattie', 'Lost', 'Mind The Gap' and ' Twin Trouble', all printed by permission of the author.

DR HEINRICH HOFFMANN (German 1809-1894):' Augustus' and 'Little Suck-a-Thumb', from *Struwwelpeter (Shockheaded Peter)* (Loenig 1845), published in England 1848, translator unknown.

DAVID HORNSBY (b. 1932): 'Tom's Bomb', from *Allsorts 6* (Methuen 1974) and *Allsorts of Poems*, (Angus & Robertson 1978) reprinted by permission of the author.

A. E. HOUSMAN (1859-1936): 'Amelia Mixed the Mustard', from *My Brother A. E. H.* by Laurence Housman (1937) reprinted by permission of The Society of Authors..

LAURENCE HOUSMAN (1865-1959): 'Word of Honour' and 'A Standing Order', from *The New Child's Guide To Knowledge*, (Sidgwick & Jackson) reprinted by permission of the Random House Group Ltd.

WALLACE IRWIN (American 1876-1959): 'Arthur', 'Nina' and 'The Education of Grandpa', from *Random Rhymes & Odd Numbers* (MacMillan Co. NY 1906)

VIOLET JACOB (Scottish 1863-1946): 'Ill-Timed Levity' and 'The Result of Heedlessness' from the *Infant Moralist* (Foulis 1926). 'Kind Aunt Mary', from *The Good Child's Year Book* (Foulis 1927).

CARA LOCKHART SMITH (b. 1945): 'Nancy', from *Riding To Canonbie*, (Hamish Hamilton 1972) reprinted by permission of the author.

EDITH F. B. MACALISTER: 'John and the Top Hat', 'Maria and the Scissors' and 'Maria and the Inks', from *The Misdeeds of Maria* (Hodder & Stoughton 1926)

FAY MASCHLER (b. 1945): 'Celia', from *A Child's Book of Manners* (Jonathan Cape 1978) reprinted by permission of the author.

IAN MCMILLAN (b. 1957) 'Natasha Green', printed by permission of the author.

OGDEN NASH (Amerian 1902-1971): 'The Boy Who Laughed at Santa Claus'. Copyright © 1942 by Ogden Nash, renewed. Reprinted by permission of Curtis Brown Ltd.

JOSEPH S. NEWMAN (b. 1891): 'Baby Kate.'

JEREMY NICHOLAS (b. 1947): 'Alexander Phillinoy', 'Cynthia Simpson',

Acknowledgements

'Mary-Jane and Emily', from *Raspberries & Other Trifles* (Hutchinson, 1984) reprinted by permission of the author.

ADELAIDE O'KEEFFE (1776-1855): 'False Alarms', from *Original Poems For Infant Minds* (Darton & Harvey, 1804).

KATHLEEN PYLE (American 1863-1938): 'Untidy Amanda' and 'The Beet', from *Careless Jane & Other Tales* (W & R Chambers, 1904).

E.V. RIEU (1887-1972): 'Two People' and 'Dirge for a Bad Boy', from *Cuckoo Calling* (Methuen, 1933) reprinted by permission Richard Rieu.

IAN SERRAILLIER (1912-1994): 'Andrew's Bedtime Story' from *Happily Ever After* (OUP 1963) reprinted by permission of Anne Serraillier.

KATHERINE E. SHERRIFF: 'Christopher Cash' from *Chatterbox Christmas Annual 1925.*

JAN STRUTHER (1901-1953): 'The Story of Anthony the Boy Who Knew Too Much', 'The Story of Cheeky Charles', 'The Story of Disobedient David', 'The Dreadful Story of Janet', 'The Story of Frozen James', 'The Story of Foolish Philip' and 'The Story of Patrick in London', by Struther and Ernest Shepard, from *The Modern Struwwelpeter*, Methuen, 1936 reprinted by permission of *Punch*.

ANN TAYLOR (1782-1866): 'The Chatterbox' and 'Meddlesome Matty', from *Original Poems for Infant Minds*, Darton & Harvey 1804

ELIZABETH TURNER (1775-1846): 'Poisonous Fruit' and 'Miss Sophia',from *The Daisy* (1806) 'Haircutting', 'The Cruel Boy', 'Fretful Phoebe' and 'Prudent Little Ned' from *The Cowslip* or *Grandma's Book of Rhymes for Children.*

W. TREGO WEBB (1847-1934): 'Augustus Flatnose', 'Mischievous Bartholemew', 'Penelope Pull-Rope', 'Philip Never-Go-To-Bed', 'Alonzo-never-shut-the-door' and 'Cruel Joe', from *A Book of Bad Children* (Methuen 1907).

CAROLYN WELLS (1862-1942): 'Mabel 1'

COLIN WEST (b. 1951): 'Adolphus', 'Clumsy Clarissa', 'Humphrey Hughes of Highbury', 'Peter', 'My Sister Sybil', 'Zachary's Progress' and 'An Alphabet of Horrible Habits', from *The Best of West*, (Hutchinson1990) reprinted by permission of the author.

ALISON WINN (b. 1909): 'Fred', 'Jonathan', and 'Richard', from *Patchwork Pieces*, Brockhampton 1980 reprinted by the permission of the author & Alison Edwards.

KIT WRIGHT (b. 1944): 'Dave Dirt Came to Dinner', from *Hot Dog and Other Poems* (Kestrel, 1981) reprinted by permission of the author.

The Naughtiest Children I Know